Tennessee
Legal Research

CAROLINA ACADEMIC PRESS
LEGAL RESEARCH SERIES

Suzanne E. Rowe, Series Editor

&

Arizona, Second Edition—Tamara S. Herrera

Arkansas, Second Edition—Coleen M. Barger, Cheryl L. Reinhart &
Cathy L. Underwood

California, Third Edition—Aimee Dudovitz, Hether C. Macfarlane,
& Suzanne E. Rowe

Colorado—Robert Michael Linz

Connecticut—Jessica G. Hynes

Federal, Second Edition—Mary Garvey Algero, Spencer L. Simons,
Suzanne E. Rowe, Scott Childs & Sarah E. Ricks

Florida, Fourth Edition—Barbara J. Busharis, Jennifer LaVia & Suzanne E. Rowe

Georgia—Nancy P. Johnson, Elizabeth G. Adelman & Nancy J. Adams

Idaho, Second Edition—Tenielle Fordyce-Ruff & Kristina J. Running

Illinois, Second Edition—Mark E. Wojcik

Iowa, Second Edition—John D. Edwards, Karen L. Wallace &
Melissa H. Weresh

Kansas—Joseph A. Custer & Christopher L. Steadham

Kentucky—William A. Hilyerd, Kurt X. Metzmeier & David J. Ensign

Louisiana, Second Edition—Mary Garvey Algero

Massachusetts, Second Edition—E. Joan Blum & Shaun B. Spencer

Michigan, Third Edition—Pamela Lysaght & Cristina D. Lockwood

Minnesota—Suzanne Thorpe

Mississippi—Kristy L. Gilliland

Missouri, Third Edition—Wanda M. Temm & Julie M. Cheslik

New York, Third Edition—Elizabeth G. Adelman, Theodora Belniak
Courtney L. Selby & Brian Detweiler

North Carolina, Second Edition—Scott Childs & Sara Sampson

North Dakota—Anne Mullins & Tammy Pettinato

Ohio, Second Edition—Sara Sampson, Katherine L. Hall
& Carolyn Broering-Jacobs

Oklahoma—Darin K. Fox, Darla W. Jackson & Courtney L. Selby

Oregon, Third Edition Revised Printing—Suzanne E. Rowe

Pennsylvania—Barbara J. Busharis & Bonny L. Tavares

Tennessee, Second Edition—Scott Childs, Sibyl Marshall & Carol McCrehan Parker

Texas, Second Edition—Spencer L. Simons

Washington, Second Edition—Julie Heintz-Cho, Tom Cobb
& Mary A. Hotchkiss

West Virginia—Hollee Schwartz Temple

Wisconsin—Patricia Cervenka & Leslie Behroozi

Wyoming, Second Edition—Debora A. Person & Tawnya K. Plumb

&

Tennessee
Legal Research

Second Edition

Scott Childs
Sibyl Marshall
Carol McCrehan Parker

Suzanne E. Rowe, Series Editor

CAROLINA ACADEMIC PRESS

Durham, North Carolina

Library of Congress Cataloging-in-Publication Data

Names: Childs, Scott, author. | Marshall, Sibyl, author. | Parker, Carol
    McCrehan, 1954- author.
Title: Tennessee legal research / Scott Childs, Sibyl Marshall, Carol
    McCrehan Parker.
Description: Second edition. | Durham, North Carolina : Carolina Academic
    Press, [2016] | Series: Legal research series | Includes bibliographical
    references and index.
Identifiers: LCCN 2016028053 | ISBN 9781611637120 (alk. paper)
Subjects: LCSH: Legal research--Tennessee.
Classification: LCC KFT75 .C45 2016 | DDC 340.072/0768--dc23
LC record available at https://lccn.loc.gov/2016028053

Carolina Academic Press, LLC
700 Kent Street
Durham, North Carolina 27701
Telephone (919) 489-7486
Fax (919) 493-5668
www.cap-press.com

Printed in the United States of America.

Summary of Contents

Contents

List of Tables and Figures

Tables

Figures

Series Note

The Legal Research Series published by Carolina Academic Press includes titles from states around the country as well as a separate text on federal legal research. The goal of each book is to provide law students, practitioners, paralegals, college students, laypeople, and librarians with the essential elements of legal research in each jurisdiction. Unlike more bibliographic texts, the Legal Research Series books seek to explain concisely both the sources of legal research and the process for conducting legal research effectively.

Preface and Acknowledgments

Significant change and important developments have occurred in the legal information world since the first edition of this book in 2007. The changes include both the continued proliferation of digital legal information sources as well as the sophistication of search engines. Sadly, less progress has been made to authenticate free or lower cost digital legal information. But the widespread availability and convenience of those sources demands that they play an increasing role in a savvy legal research process.

We discuss these recent changes to existing legal information sources in the second edition, while also acknowledging some of the newer sources. As with the first edition, this edition focuses on the use of these sources in a coherent research process we believe is uniquely tailored for researching legal issues in Tennessee.

Tennessee Legal Research was not developed in a vacuum. The first edition drew significantly from previous work by the Series Editor, Suzanne Rowe, and her book, *Oregon Legal Research*. A number of other people were involved, in addition to Suzanne, in editing and crafting the original text. Although many of these people identified in the preface to the first edition have moved along or retired, their original and valuable contributions remain reflected here in the second edition.

In addition to those people playing important roles in the development and publication of the first edition, new contributors and facilitators have been added along the way to the publication of this second edition. First, Scott Childs, Associate Dean for Library and Technology Services at the University of Tennessee College of Law Library, joins us as a new co-author to this edition. His perspective from co-authoring, with Sara Sampson, a recent second edition of *North Carolina Legal Research* is reflected in this work and some areas of several chapters are drawn from it. Of course, much gratitude is owed again to series editor, Suzanne Rowe, for her work also editing this second edition and making this edition possible. University of Tennessee law student Andrew

Tucker also made valuable contributions and recommendations for this edition. Finally, we wish to thank the faculty and staff of the University of Tennessee College of Law Library for their support during the writing of this book.

Tennessee
Legal Research

Chapter 1

The Research Process and Legal Analysis

I. Tennessee Legal Research[1]

The fundamentals of legal research are the same in every American juris-diction, though the details vary, due to either unique legal structures or sources of law. While some variations are minor, others require specialized knowledge of the legal structures and sources of law in a jurisdiction before beginning the research process. This book examines the process of legal research required to be thorough and efficient in researching Tennessee law. Throughout the book, the examination of researching the law in Tennessee will be supplemented with brief discussions of researching federal law. On occasion, the ability to research federal law may be an important element of competently researching a legal issue arising in Tennessee. In a few instances, reference to researching the law of other states may be discussed for the purpose of highlighting differences.

II. The Intersection of Legal Research and Legal Analysis

The basic process of legal research is simple; however, legal analysis is in-terwoven throughout this process, raising challenging questions. This book promotes a process-centered approach to legal research. Although the book will discuss structures of the Tennessee legal system and the sources of law produced by that legal system, it will also address how the use of these sources fits into a broad process of researching.

Legal analysis drives the research process. For example, most online research involves the familiar process of searching particular websites or databases using words likely to appear in the text of relevant documents, but how will you

---

1. This part of the chapter draws from *Oregon Legal Research* and is used with per-mission.

3

choose those words? What words will you use to search for law addressing the legal concepts you are researching? When you find primary law, how will you know what it means and how it applies to your issue or question? If you find a case that is relevant, how will you know whether law created after the case was decided changes how the case might be interpreted? These questions all involve legal analysis.

The intersection of research and analysis can make legal research very difficult, especially for the novice. As your understanding of legal analysis deepens, the process of legal research will become both easier and more efficient. While this book's focus is legal research, it also includes the fundamental aspects of legal analysis required to conduct research competently. This book is not designed to be a blueprint of every resource in the law library or search engine on the Internet. Instead, it is more like a manual or field guide, introducing the types of resources needed at each step of the research process and explaining how to use them.

III. Types of Legal Authority

Before researching the law, you must be clear about the goal of your search. The goal might be to answer a specific question. A different goal might be to develop a broader understanding of a particular area of law. Whatever the goal might be, as a researcher, you usually will seek information or a specific answer that is authoritative.

Legal authority may be divided along two lines: primary and secondary. *Primary authority* is produced by government bodies with law-making power, and it *is* the law. By contrast, *secondary authorities* are materials that are written *about* the law. Secondary authorities include treatises, law review articles, and legal encyclopedias. Secondary authorities are designed to aid researchers both in understanding the law and in locating primary authorities.[2]

A. Primary Authority

Primary authority is law issued by bodies constitutionally authorized to pronounce the law. The legislature adopts statutes requiring or prohibiting actions. The executive branch enforces these laws by promulgating detailed regulations prescribing exactly how these statutes must be implemented and

---

2. A third type of legal material is the *tertiary authority* or "finding aid." These materials consist entirely of tables, indexes, digests, and citators. They are used entirely for locating primary and secondary authorities.

enforcing the laws. When legal disputes arise, judges hear arguments and issue decisions settling the disputes. All of these institutions—the legislature, the executive branch, and the courts—are issuing primary law. Primary authority may be either *mandatory* or *persuasive*.

1. Mandatory Authority

Mandatory authority is binding on the court that would decide a conflict if the situation were litigated. Primary law from the jurisdiction where a legal issue arises is called primary, mandatory authority.[3] It is primary because of the body that issued it. It is mandatory because it was issued by institutions of the jurisdiction where the question arose and it is the law that must be applied. In a question of Tennessee law, mandatory (or binding), primary authority includes Tennessee's constitution, statutes enacted by the Tennessee legislature, Tennessee administrative regulations, and opinions of the Tennessee Supreme Court.[4] In most situations, you will be looking for authority that is both primary and mandatory.

Within primary, mandatory authority, there is an interlocking hierarchy of law involving constitutions, statutes, procedural rules, administrative regulations, and judicial opinions. The constitution of each state is the supreme law of that state. If a statute is on point, that statute comes next in the hierarchy, followed by administrative regulations and procedural rules. Courts determine whether statutes, regulations, and rules violate the constitution and will strike down any law, regulation, or rule found to be unconstitutional. Courts are also responsible for interpreting statutes, regulations, and rules as well as ensuring that regulations and rules do not contradict statutes. If there is no constitutional provision, statute, administrative regulation, or procedural rule on point, the issue will be controlled by *common law* or judge-made law.

2. Persuasive Authority

Primary authority that is issued by legislatures, administrative agencies, or courts from other state jurisdictions—outside of the jurisdiction where the

---

3. Case law is only mandatory if it is from a higher court within the jurisdiction. It must also be on point, the part of the opinion under discussion must be holding rather than dicta, and no later law may have changed it.

4. An opinion from the Tennessee Court of Criminal Appeals or the Tennessee Court of Appeals is binding on the Tennessee trial courts if the Tennessee Supreme Court has not addressed a particular issue. The Tennessee Supreme Court's earlier opinions are not binding on future cases decided by that court, though that court may choose to follow them under the doctrine of *stare decisis*.

legal issue being researched arose—is called primary, persuasive authority. This authority is primary because of the nature of the body issuing it, but only persuasive because it was not issued from a legal body of the relevant jurisdiction. While primary, persuasive authority is not mandatory outside of the jurisdiction in which it was issued, it might be persuasive when there is no existing primary, mandatory authority in a jurisdiction. In a question of Tennessee law, examples of primary, persuasive authority include a similar Georgia statute and an opinion of a Kentucky state court.

B. Secondary Authority

In contrast to primary authority issued by legal bodies within a jurisdiction, secondary authority is commentary on or description of the law, typically written by law professors, legal practitioners, or editors from legal publishers. While there are levels of authoritativeness within the category of secondary authority, it is not the law. Therefore, secondary authority is always treated as persuasive, never mandatory. Table 1-1 shows examples of different types of authorities in Tennessee research.

Table 1-1. Examples of Authority in Tennessee Research

	Mandatory Authority	Persuasive Authority
Primary Authority	Tennessee statutes	Georgia statutes
	Tennessee Supreme Court cases	Kentucky Supreme Court cases
Secondary Authority	—————	Law review articles
		Legal encyclopedias
		Treatises

IV. Court Systems

Because much legal research includes reading judicial opinions, researchers need to understand the court system. The basic court structure includes a trial court, an intermediate court of appeals, and an ultimate appellate court, often called the "supreme" court. These court systems exist at both the state and federal levels.

In the typical court structure for most states and the federal judicial system in the United States, the trial court is the basic court where most legal issues are initiated and resolved. Often, more trivial or magisterial matters such as traffic violations or small claims matters may even be initiated below the trial court level. In addition to the basic trial courts, many states have specialized trial courts that address specific areas, such as family law or drug-related crimes, where a court's particular subject expertise is important.

While the vast majority of litigation is concluded at the trial court level, most of the trial court decisions do not have precedential value because of the trial courts' low level in the court system hierarchy; therefore, these decisions are not useful for research purposes. State trial court decisions, Tennessee's included, are typically not widely available and often may not be accompanied by written opinions. Trial court opinions at the federal level are only slightly more available and still suffer from a similar lack of research usefulness due to their low level in the federal court system hierarchy.

When researching case law, particularly in state jurisdictions, you will usually be researching appellate cases. In most state court systems as well as the federal court system, there is an intermediate appellate court, and an ultimate or supreme appellate court.

A. Tennessee Courts

Tennessee has four different types of trial level courts. Where a case will first be heard may depend on the type of case, the amount of damages sought, or the county where it is filed, as not all counties have all types of courts. *Circuit courts* are the most common type of trial courts, and they hear certain civil matters, domestic relations cases, and criminal cases. *Chancery courts* hear some family law cases and those civil cases that are traditionally considered to arise from equity rather than law.[5] The jurisdiction of the chancery courts is varied and includes cases arising out of boundary disputes, demands for specific performance of a contract, and suits by wards against their guardians. *Criminal courts* hear exclusively criminal cases, and *Probate courts* hear cases involving wills, administration of estates, conservatorships, and guardianships.

In addition to these state trial courts, Tennessee has county trial courts. Courts of *limited jurisdiction* are trial courts that typically hear smaller cases and are funded at the county level rather than the state level. In Tennessee,

---

5. Equity is a body of law that developed to address concerns outside of the traditional jurisdiction of common law. Equity law cases were traditionally heard in chancery courts. For more about chancery courts in Tennessee, see *Gibson's Suits in Chancery*, 8th ed. (William H. Inman rev., LexisNexis 2014) which is considered the definitive work on theory of and practice in Tennessee chancery courts.

courts of limited jurisdiction include Juvenile courts, General Sessions courts, and Municipal courts. *Juvenile courts* hear cases involving juveniles, including paternity cases, mental health cases, and juvenile delinquency cases. *General Sessions courts* handle preliminary hearings in criminal cases, small claims matters, traffic violations, and some civil and misdemeanor criminal matters. *Municipal courts* deal with preliminary hearings, traffic violations, and other misdemeanor criminal violations. Again, not every county will have all of these different types of courts.

Tennessee has two intermediate courts of appeal. The *Court of Criminal Appeals* hears appeals in criminal cases and is required to review all death penalty sentences. The *Court of Appeals* hears appeals in civil cases, as well as taking appeals from certain state boards and commissions. Both intermediate courts are composed of twelve judges, who sit in panels of three in Jackson, Nashville, and Knoxville.

The *Tennessee Supreme Court* is composed of five justices, who sit *en banc* to hear all cases. The Supreme Court also convenes regularly in Jackson, Nashville, and Knoxville.[6] The Supreme Court decides which appeals it wants to hear and is only required to review those cases where the Court of Criminal Appeals has affirmed a death sentence. The Supreme Court may also choose to assume jurisdiction over cases in the Court of Appeals or Court of Criminal Appeals if there is a particular need for a swift resolution.

The website for the Tennessee judiciary includes searchable databases of Tennessee court opinions, links to procedural rules and the Tennessee code, contact information for Tennessee court clerks, court forms, court programs, a self-help center, an extensive section of links to external sources on Tennessee and American law, and a series of streaming videos on basic court procedures, offered in seven languages.[7]

B. Federal Courts

In the federal judicial system, the trial courts are called the *United States District Courts*. There are ninety-four district courts in the federal system, with each state having at least one district. A state with a relatively small population may have only one district. The entire state of South Carolina, for example,

---

6. Although the Court of Criminal Appeals, Court of Appeals, and Supreme Court usually are held in traditional court buildings, the courts do occasionally convene and hear argument outside of the usual courtrooms — usually at Tennessee law schools.

7. The address is www.tsc.state.tn.us.

makes up the federal District of South Carolina. States with larger populations and higher caseloads are subdivided into more districts. Tennessee has three federal districts: Eastern, Middle, and Western. Mississippi has two federal districts: Northern and Southern.

Intermediate appellate courts in the federal system are called the *United States Courts of Appeals.* There are courts of appeals for each of the thirteen federal circuits. Twelve of these circuits are based on geographic jurisdiction. Eleven numbered circuits cover all the states, and the District of Columbia Circuit is the twelfth geographic federal circuit court of appeals. The thirteenth federal circuit, called the Federal Circuit, hears appeals from district courts in all other circuits on issues related to patent law and from certain specialized courts and agencies.[8] A map showing the federal circuits and underlying districts is available at the US Courts website.[9]

Tennessee is in the Sixth Circuit. This means that cases from the Western, Middle, and Eastern District Courts of Tennessee are appealed to the Court of Appeals for the Sixth Circuit. This circuit encompasses Michigan, Ohio, and Kentucky, in addition to Tennessee.

The highest court in the federal system is the *United States Supreme Court.* It decides cases concerning the United States Constitution and federal statutes. This court does not have the final say on matters of purely state law; that authority rests with the highest court of each state. Parties who wish to have the United States Supreme Court hear their case must file a petition for *certiorari,* as the court has discretion over which cases it hears.

C. Courts of Other States

Most states have the three-tier court system of Tennessee and the federal judiciary, though a few states do not have an intermediate appellate court. Tennessee is one of only four states that have separate appellate courts to handle criminal and civil matters.[10] Another difference in some court systems is that the "supreme" court is not the highest court. In New York, trial courts are called supreme courts and the highest court is the Court of Appeals. Two other states, Massachusetts and Maine, call their highest court the Supreme Judicial Court.

8. For more information about this court, see United States Court of Appeals for the Federal Circuit, http://cafc.uscourts.gov/ .http://fedcir.gov/about.html
9. The map on the US Courts website is available at http://www.uscourts.gov/file/documents/us-federal-courts-circuit-map.
10. The other three states are Alabama, Oklahoma, and Texas.

Citation manuals are good references for learning the names and hierarchies of different court systems, as well as for learning proper citation to legal authorities. The two most popular are *The Bluebook: A Uniform System of Citation*, which is written by students from several law schools,[11] and the *ALWD Guide to Legal Citation*, written by Professor Coleen Barger and the Association of Legal Writing Directors.[12] Table T1 of the *Bluebook* and Appendix 1 of the *ALWD Guide* provide information on federal and state courts.

V. Overview of the Research Process

A. The Basic Process

Conducting effective legal research means following a process. This process leads to the authority that controls a legal issue as well as to commentary that may help you analyze new and complex legal matters. The outline in Table 1-2 presents the basic research process.

Table 1-2. Overview of the Research Process

1. Generate a list of *research terms* (also called *keywords*).

2. Consult *secondary authorities* such as practice manuals, treatises, legal encyclopedias, and law review articles. Note new research terms and any citations to primary authorities that appear relevant.

3. Find controlling *constitutional provisions, statutes, regulations,* or *court rules* by searching online databases or reviewing print indexes, using your research terms as modified by your review of secondary authorities. Read these authorities carefully, and study the annotations to find cross-references to additional authorities and explanatory materials.

4. Find citations to relevant case law by reading annotations in statutory codes, searching online databases, or using *digests.* A digest is essentially a multi-volume topic index of cases in a certain jurisdiction or subject area.

5. Read the cases fully and carefully, either online or in a *reporter.* A reporter series publishes the full text of cases, in roughly chronological order, in a certain jurisdiction or subject area.

6. *Update* your primary authorities by using a citator such as Shepard's, KeyCite, or BCite. Updating will let you know whether your authorities are still good

---

11. *The Bluebook: A Uniform System of Citation* (Columbia Law Review Ass'n et al. eds., 20th ed. 2015). This book's citations conform to the *Bluebook.*

12. Ass'n of Legal Writing Directors & Coleen M. Barger, *ALWD Guide to Legal Citation* (5th ed. 2014).

law or if they have been repealed, reversed, modified, or otherwise changed. Updating will also help you find additional relevant authorities.

7. Know you are finished when you *encounter the same authorities* and no new authorities through all the research methods you employ.

This basic process should be customized for each research project. Consider whether you need to follow all seven steps, and if so, in what order. If you are unfamiliar with an area of law, you should follow each step in the order indicated, making certain to start with secondary authorities. Beginning with secondary authorities will provide both context for the issues you must research and citations to relevant primary authority. As you gain experience in researching legal questions, you may choose to modify the process. For example, if you know that a situation is controlled by the common law, you may choose to skip looking for statutes and rules.

B. Generating Research Terms

Online legal sources often require the researcher to enter words that are likely to appear in a synopsis or in the full text of relevant documents. Alternatively, many print legal resources use lengthy indexes of concepts or topics as the starting point for finding legal authority. To ensure you are thorough in beginning a research project, you will need a comprehensive list of words, terms, and phrases that may lead to law on point. These may be legal terms or common words that describe the client's situation. The items on this list are *research terms*, which are often called *keywords*.

Organized brainstorming is the best way to compile a comprehensive list of research terms. Some researchers ask the journalistic questions: Who? What? How? Why? When? Where? Others use a mnemonic device like TARPP, which stands for Things, Actions, Remedies, People, and Places.[13] Whether you use one of these suggestions or develop your own method, generate a broad range of research terms regarding the facts, issues, and desired solutions of your client's situation. Include in the list both specific and general words. Try to think of synonyms and antonyms for each term. Using a legal dictionary or thesaurus may help generate terms.

How you use the terms in online searching is different from how you use them in print research. In online searching you will most often use these words

---

13. *See* Stephen M. Barkan, Roy M. Mersky and Donald J. Dunn, *Fundamentals of Legal Research* (10th ed. 2015) (explaining "TARP," a similar mnemonic device).

to search the full text of documents. This is called "full-text" searching. There can be disadvantages with this search method. If the author of a particular document does not use the exact term you are searching for, you will not find that document in your results.

By contrast, in print, you look for the terms in indexes and tables of contents to find relevant portions of books. Sometimes this is referred to as "conceptual research" because you are searching indexes for concepts that lawyers have used over time to describe a cause of action, defense, or remedy.

As an example, assume you are working for a defense attorney who was recently assigned to a burglary case. Around midnight, your client allegedly bent a credit card to spring the lock to a stereo store, where she is accused of having stolen $2,000 worth of equipment. She was charged with first-degree burglary. You have been asked to determine whether there is a good argument for limiting the charge to second-degree burglary based on the fact that she used a credit card and not professional burglar tools. Table 1-3 provides examples of research terms you might use to begin work on this project.

Table 1-3. Generating Research Terms

Journalistic Approach

Who: Thief, robber, burglar

What: Burglary, first degree, second degree, crime

How: Breaking and entering, burglar tools, trespassing, credit card

Why: Theft, stealing, burglary, rob, stolen goods

When: Midnight, night

Where: Store, building, shop, commercial establishment

TARPP Approach

Things: Burglar tool, credit card

Actions: Burglary, breaking and entering, trespassing, crime, using credit card to spring lock

Remedies: First degree, second degree

People: Burglar, thief, robber

Places: Store, building, commercial establishment, business, shop

After compiling your initial list of research terms, scan through and pick out the ones that appear most frequently and that you believe are the most important. Use those as your starting point. Remember that as your research progresses, you will learn new research terms to include in the list, and decide to take others off. For example, by reading secondary authorities, you may learn a *term of art*, a word or phrase that has special meaning in a particular area of law. Also, remember to return to your list of research terms during your research process in order to refine your research. If you try an online search using words like "burglary," "second degree," and "burglar tools" and get inundated with far too many results, reviewing your list of terms to find something more specific, such as "credit card," might help you significantly narrow and focus your potential list of cases to read.

C. Researching the Law — Basic Strategies for Research in Online Sources[14]

The use of online resources is critically important when conducting efficient and effective legal research in today's environment. The following explanation of basic online research strategies lays the foundation for understanding discussions of researching specific types of legal information in later chapters.

1. Overview of Commercial Research Services

The three largest and most comprehensive commercial providers of online legal information are Thomson Reuters Westlaw, LexisNexis, and Bloomberg Law. Two of those services, Westlaw and Lexis, have been serving the legal community for decades, greatly expanding access to legal information and evolving over the years with the changing technology. Bloomberg Law is a newcomer to the legal information field, but has developed an impressive array of features and content.

Westlaw is owned by Thomson Reuters and provides nearly comprehensive access to legal information. Periodically, the Westlaw search engine and interface change due to technological advances. As of the writing of this book, the most recent version of the Westlaw research product was released in 2010; originally called WestlawNext, in 2016 the name was changed to Westlaw. It presents a universal search bar in which you may enter keywords, natural-language-type phrases, or known citations. The site provides substantial browsability, enabling a more sophisticated researcher to select specific databases within which to browse or search.

LexisNexis is a Reed Elsevier product, also providing nearly comprehensive access to legal information. The most recent version of the LexisNexis research

---

14. This part of the chapter draws from *North Carolina Legal Research* and is used with permission.

product is Lexis Advance, released in 2011. Lexis Advance presents a universal search bar in which you may enter keywords, natural-language-type phrases, or known citations. Although Lexis Advance currently provides less browsability than Westlaw does, Lexis Advance regularly provides updates to its interfaces that typically include more browsability and advanced search features being added in. This book's discussion of Lexis will focus exclusively on the Lexis Advance product.

Bloomberg Law is a 2010 product of Bloomberg L.P., a publisher long known and respected for company and market information and related news. Bloomberg Law acquired Bureau of National Affairs (BNA) in 2011. Bloomberg's ability to provide sophisticated and comprehensive legal news as well as an array of commentary, analysis, and primary law was greatly enhanced through the BNA products. Like Westlaw and Lexis Advance, the Bloomberg Law interface also presents a single search bar for instant searching with keywords; however, it currently does not support natural-language searching.

Although distinctions exist between the services, Westlaw and Lexis products each approach near comprehensiveness in content and share many common strategies for efficient use. While Bloomberg Law may lack in overall comprehensiveness, it excels at providing extensive litigation and transactional resources, including superior access to court filing and litigation tracking. Bloomberg Law also has excellent access to legal news, legal current awareness services, and financial and business materials.

Generally, the explanations of online search strategies in this section apply specifically to those three services. Major differences will be identified. Although prices vary depending upon specific uses, these three services are expensive. A growing number of less expensive fee-based alternatives exist, generally providing primary legal information with substantially fewer editorial enhancements and fewer secondary sources of legal information. Of most interest in Tennessee is Fastcase, which is provided free as part of membership in the Tennessee Bar Association. In addition, some government websites provide free access to basic and recent primary law.

2. Using Known Citations to Locate Specific Documents

You may retrieve a document on Westlaw, Lexis Advance, or Bloomberg Law by entering a known citation — typically including a volume number, a publication abbreviation, and a page number — into the universal search bar. This feature is effective for retrieving cases, journal articles, statutory provisions, and administrative code sections.

3. Browsing Online

One of the great improvements in the last decade in researching with online information is the increasing availability of browsing online. Online browsability adds the advantage of reading in context that is common in print publications. Westlaw, Lexis Advance, and Bloomberg Law all allow you to browse to find a particular source or discussion, rather than using the universal search bar. Once you find a particular source, you may be able to browse to a particular part of it, often by using an online table of contents. Once you find a relevant part of the source, such as a statute or an in-depth discussion in a treatise, you may be able to use "Next page" and "Previous page" buttons to continue reading in the same manner as you would with a print book, rather than searching or using hyperlinks to navigate.

4. Key Number Digest of Case Law on Westlaw

Over 400 topics, subdivided into thousands of sub-topics, are available on Westlaw. This is the currently updated contents of the entire West Digest System developed over 100 years ago, available online. Browsing the digest is a complex task for new researchers and will be more fully discussed in Chapter 2.

5. Key Word Searching

a. Methods and Strategies for Full-text Key Word Searching

Keyword searching, sometimes called terms and connectors (or Boolean logic) searching, allows the most control over an online search. Using terms and connectors allows you to construct very specific searches. A few examples are given in Table 1-4.

Each service has slightly different terms and connectors operators. Make sure you check for these operators before searching, unless you are quite familiar with the service and its search options. Also, be careful and flexible when con-

Table 1-4. Sample Terms and Connectors Searches

Apartment w/3 pets	Retrieves all documents with the words *apartment* and *pets* within three words of each other.
Apartment w/3 (pets or cat or dog or bird)	Retrieves all documents with the word *apartment* within three words of any of the words *pets*, *cat*, *dog*, or *bird*.
Apartment w/s leas!	Retrieves all documents with the word *apartment* in the same sentence as any word starting with *leas*: lease, leases, leasing, etc.
Apartment w/p "right of inspection"	Retrieves all documents with the word *apartment* in the same paragraph as the exact phrase *right of inspection*.

structing your searches. In the third example in Table 1-4, you would retrieve documents not just with *lease* or *leases* but also with *leash* and *leashes*, which may not be exactly what you want!

Generally, Westlaw and Lexis Advance will perform terms and connectors searching if you enter terms with connectors. Otherwise, those services will default to natural-language searching with the search terms you enter. Bloomberg Law will only perform terms and connector searching and does not provide natural-language searching at this time. Natural-language searching is discussed below in Section 6.

Using the terms and connector searching method, you first identify search terms as previously discussed. When searching full text, it's important to think of all the various ways your terms might have been described by the authors of every document in the database you search. For example, in a case law database, there are many individual authors (judges) of the cases in the database. What language did each of them use to describe your search terms? The fewer the possibilities there are, the more likely you are to retrieve all of the relevant documents.

After identifying search terms, you next define the relationships between the search terms using connectors. Phrase searching is a particularly specific method of searching, especially when the phrase is a term of art or a search term most likely to appear in all relevant documents. All of the services require the words in a phrase to be included within quotation marks to be searched as a phrase using the Boolean search method.

In addition to the relationship established between two terms by each connector, there is a default order in which two or more connectors are processed in each search. The order in which connectors are processed may greatly affect the outcome of the search. The general default order of processing follows this sequence: "phrase," OR, w/n, w/s, w/p, AND, But Not (And Not).

EXAMPLE: apartment w/3 lease and pets or dogs

Since the OR connector is processed first in this search, the system would begin by locating documents with either *pets* or *dogs* anywhere in the text. Next, the system would locate documents where *apartment* is found within three words of *lease*. Finally, the system would combine the requirements to retrieve only those documents that contained either *pets* or *dogs* as long as *apartment* was within three words of *lease* in each document.

You may change this default order of processing by placing parentheses around the parts of your search that you want processed first. Terms and connectors within parentheses will be processed first—in the default order listed above—and then the terms and connectors outside of the parentheses will be processed.

A common online search strategy is to begin your search in the smallest database that you know will contain all the relevant documents. For example, if you are searching for Tennessee cases, select a database that has only Tennessee cases rather than one including cases from all fifty states. Once you have selected the smallest database you believe will contain all of the relevant documents, initiate a broad, inclusive search.

After formulating and running a search, you must evaluate the results that the search retrieves. Typically, you should contemplate additional refining based upon the effectiveness of the search and incorporating what you learned in the initial search. For this initial broad-search approach, Westlaw, Lexis Advance, and Bloomberg Law all have a feature allowing you to filter the initial retrieved set of documents by jurisdiction, source or type of information, etc., depending upon the contents of the database. Look for these options when viewing a retrieved set of search results. These types of filters may have the additional benefit of not incurring additional charges for those customers paying transactional costs or using per-search pricing.

b. Keyword Searching an Online Index Database

For a few large databases of information where a print index already exists, Westlaw and Lexis Advance provide a separate database containing just the index that may be searched or browsed. This feature brings the advantage of a human-analyzed set of search terms identified from within the database and associated with their locations within each document. The index databases may include a search engine or simply be a browsable list of all the index terms as would be found in the print index. Using the index database might be an excellent way to approach a code of statutory law, such as the *Tennessee Code Annotated*, rather than using a full-text keyword search of the entire code database.

c. Keyword Searching a Field or Segment of Each Document in a Database

Field searching is a feature allowing researchers to limit their search to just certain parts of each document in a database rather than searching each word of every document. For example, if you are trying to find a particular case in a database and have a party's name, you can search just the part of all the cases in the database that includes party names. Field searching might also be an effective search strategy to use when trying to locate all the decisions written by a particular judge. You could limit your search to just the "judge" field of each case in the database and use the judge's name as the search term. By limiting the search to just that field, you would not retrieve cases that mention this judge's name in the text, only those actually authored by the judge.

Field searching is usually only available on the more expensive online services and is less common in free databases on government websites. Westlaw and Lexis Advance provides this option using the "advanced" link, near the universal search bar. Bloomberg Law provides this option at the bottom of the typical search screen; it can usually be found by simply scrolling down the screen. You can also use post-search filtering options on all of these services to achieve similar results.

6. Natural-Language Searching

Natural-language searching allows you to enter search terms without connectors. Just as you would with common search engines, you may enter ask a question summarizing the issue you are researching: *are "three strikes" laws constitutional?* Or *does the clergy-penitent privilege bar testimony in Tennessee?* The system's software uses algorithms to determine which words in your search are the most important and which documents in the database are most relevant to your terms. While you have little control over the search, sometimes this approach may be useful if you are having difficulty retrieving relevant documents with a keyword search. Also, retrieved documents are automatically ranked by relevancy in a natural-language search.[15] If you need just a few relevant documents, natural-language searching can be extremely helpful. At the present, Bloomberg Law only provides the more sophisticated terms and connectors searching, and does not support natural-language searching.

D. Researching the Law — Basic Strategies for Research in Print Sources

Basic legal analysis has been intertwined with print sources of legal information for generations of lawyers and legal researchers.[16] The following strategies for using print resources take advantage of the connection between legal analysis and print resources.

---

15. In keyword searching, documents are typically presented with the most recent first, rather than those the system has determined to be most relevant to your search terms.

16. This connection was largely due to the West Digest System and the topic and key number outline of American case law, first developed in the late 1800s. In order to locate cases, researchers had to analyze the legal issues within the framework of the digest system. Much value still remains in the digest system today, which explains why it is still available both in print as well as on Westlaw.

1. Using Known Citations or Names to Locate Specific Documents

Retrieving a document with a known citation is the easiest approach to finding information in print (or online for that matter). You may know a citation because the assigning attorney gave you a citation or your previous research identified citations for you to retrieve. The general three-part nomenclature for a legal citation is the volume number, abbreviation of the title of the source, and the page or section number within that volume where the relevant document may be found. Table 2-1 of the next chapter explains in detail a case citation.

2. Browsing Tables of Contents

At the beginning of most books is a table of contents explaining how information in that publication is divided and where specific information might be found inside. Scanning the table of contents for relevant search terms is a quick way of locating the information, especially when using broader search terms. The table of contents may provide references to page numbers, section numbers, or paragraph numbers.

The other important role for tables of contents in legal research is the opportunity to see relevant information in relation to the other similar information in the publication. Seeing this analytical overview informs the researcher of potentially relevant information not yet identified or confirms the appropriateness of the information being sought. For example, scanning the table of contents of a "topic" in a case law digest provides an opportunity for additional legal analysis where you can review all of the potentially relevant sub-topics within that topic. Scanning a legal encyclopedia's table of contents provides the same opportunity to see the broader view of the subject you are researching.

3. Browsing an Index for a Specific Legal Term

The more obvious approach to print sources of law is to browse the index for your search terms. The index provides specific places in the text where the terms appear, referenced by page number, section number, or paragraph number. The index is typically located at the end of a publication, whether a single-volume or multiple-volume publication.

Indexes are more specific than tables of contents. Rather than providing an overview of a publication's content, the index is an alphabetical list of all the important terms in the publication. Because it is specific and detailed, an index typically includes some related terms that are similar to, but not necessarily found in, those terms in the documents. These cross-references direct you from your own search terms to the indexed search terms from the document; the indexed terms will lead you to the document.

4. Browsing Pocket Parts and Supplements to Update

Hardbound, law-related books are in constant need of updating. Most bound, legal publications are updated with pocket parts. These are periodic supplements (usually published annually) that are placed in a back pocket of each volume of a publication. Pocket parts may be found in single-volume books or multi-volume series, where each volume should have a pocket part. The importance of reviewing the pocket part cannot be overstated. Whatever material you reviewed in the main text should also be reviewed in the pocket part to find any changes in the law affecting this subject. If a pocket part becomes too large to fit within the cover of a volume, a free-standing pamphlet version of the pocket part is published to be shelved beside the hardbound volume. It is used in the same manner. Pocket parts or pamphlets will contain the most recent information available in print. Note that many secondary resources that are available online may only be as current as the most recent paper pocket part or pamphlet for that title.

Occasionally, a set of books may have a free-standing pamphlet instead of or in addition to pocket parts. For example, the *Tennessee Code Annotated* is updated both by annual pocket parts as well as by quarterly or semi-annual pamphlets. Likewise, the *United States Code Annotated* is updated with annual pocket parts and quarterly pamphlets.

E. Organization of This Text

The remainder of this book explains how to use your research terms to conduct legal research in a variety of sources. The book begins with primary authority because understanding primary authorities, their structure and organization, is critical to legal research and analysis, and because locating primary authority is the ultimate goal of legal research. Chapter 2 addresses the structure and format of case opinions and reporters, as well as different ways to research case law by topic. Chapter 3 describes constitutions, statutory law, procedural rules, and how to research them, with Chapter 4 giving specific guidance in performing legislative history research. Chapter 5 addresses administrative law. After this focus on finding primary authority, the following chapters explain how and why to update primary authority using citators such as Shepard's and KeyCite (Chapter 6) and how to use secondary authorities (Chapter 7). Although secondary authorities are covered later in the book, keep in mind that legal researchers often begin their research with secondary materials, especially when researching new or complex areas of law.

Chapter 8 discusses research strategies as well as how to organize your research. You may prefer to skim that chapter now and refer to it frequently, even though a number of references in it may not become clear until you are more acquainted with legal research resources and their use.

Appendix A provides a summary to finding Tennessee law in print and online. Appendix B contains a selected bibliography of texts on legal research and analysis. The general research texts tend to concentrate on federal sources, supplementing this book's brief introduction to those resources.

Chapter 2

Judicial Opinions

This chapter begins by introducing the basics of judicial opinions and the books that publish those opinions, called *reporters*. Next the chapter describes the print and online sources of state and federal judicial opinions in Tennessee, as well as the opinions of other state courts. The chapter also describes important features of published cases such as the synopsis and headnotes added by publishers as editorial enhancements. The last half of the chapter addresses how to research cases in print and online, with a particular focus on finding cases by topic, and concludes with a discussion of reading and analyzing the cases you have found.

I. Case Reporters

A judicial opinion, also informally called a *case*, is written by a court to explain its decision in a particular dispute. Cases are published in rough chronological order in books called *reporters*. Some reporters include only cases decided by a certain court, for example, the United States Supreme Court, or a system of courts, for example, all Tennessee state courts. Other reporters include cases from courts within a specific geographic region, such as the south-central United States.[1] Reporters that publish cases from a particular court or geographic area are the most commonly used by most lawyers and are the focus of this chapter.

A. Reporters and Sources for Tennessee Judicial Opinions

Since 1972, all case opinions designated for publication by Tennessee appellate courts have been published in the *South Western Reporter*.[2] The *South Western*

---

1. Still other reporters publish only those cases that deal with a particular topic, such as bankruptcy, education, or rules of civil procedure.
2. *See* 230 Tenn. at p. vi, 496 S.W.2d at p. vi (1972) (ordering publication in the *South Western Reporter*); *see also* Tenn. Sup. Ct. R. 4(A)(1) (2015).

Reporter also includes opinions from Arkansas, Kentucky, Missouri, and Texas state courts. Although it is a reporter published by the West Publishing Company, as part of its national reporter system (as opposed to being published by the government), Tennessee cases published in the *South Western Reporter* are "official" sources of law, since the state government has designated that reporter as the official publisher.[3] Table 2-1 shows how to read a case citation from the *South Western Reporter* and locate the opinion in the reporter set.

Table 2-1. Quick Guide to Decoding Citations to the *South Western Reporter*

Presley v. Memphis, 769 S.W.2d 221 (Tenn. 1988).

The abbreviation for the *South Western Reporter* is "S.W." This opinion can be found in volume 769 of the *South Western Reporter, Second Series*, starting on page 221.The case was decided in 1988. The "Tenn." designation informs the reader that this is a Tennessee case, rather than one from Texas or another state whose opinions are included in the *South Western Reporter*.

NOTE: Sometimes when a reporter reaches a certain volume number, the publisher begins another *series*. In 1927, after the publication of volume 300 of the first series, the publisher decided to begin again with volume one of the second series. The *South Western Reporter* is currently in the third series.

These citations to reporters are also used for retrieving cases from online databases. Typing "769 SW2d 221" into the search box on Westlaw, Lexis Advance, or Bloomberg Law will retrieve the full text of the *Presley v. Memphis* opinion.

Tennessee case opinions included in the *South Western Reporter* are from the Tennessee Supreme Court, the Tennessee Court of Appeals (the civil intermediate appellate court), and the Tennessee Court of Criminal Appeals. *Tennessee Decisions* is an associated reporter which reprints the Tennessee opinions from the *South Western Reporter* without the opinions from the other states.

Prior to 1972, Tennessee case opinions were also found in reporters published by the state government. Tennessee Supreme Court opinions were published in the *Tennessee Reports* (abbreviated Tenn.), Court of Appeals opinions in the *Tennessee Appeals Reports* (abbreviated Tenn. App.), and Court of Criminal Appeals opinions in the *Tennessee Criminal Appeals Reports* (abbreviated Tenn. Crim. App.).

To further complicate matters, many early volumes of the *Tennessee Reports* are commonly referred to and cited by the name of the person who held the title of "court reporter." For example, the case *Allison v. Allison* may be cited

---

3. West's national reporter system is discussed more throughout this chapter.

as 9 Tenn. (1 Yer.) 16 (1820). This means that the case can be found at volume nine, page sixteen of the *Tennessee Reports*, which is also the first volume of *Tennessee Reports* published by Mr. Yerger, the court reporter. In some instances, the citation may be given as *Allison v. Allison*, 9 Yer. 16 (Tenn. 1860). The easiest way to decipher old citation formats involving the names of court reporters is to compare them against Table T1 of *The Bluebook: A Uniform System of Citation*, which includes a list of all Tennessee Supreme Court reporters and the abbreviations associated with them.

Other older reporter series for Tennessee include Shannon's *Tennessee Cases with Notes and Annotations* (a three-volume set of edited, annotated, and otherwise unpublished Supreme Court cases from the 1870s through the 1890s), *Tennessee Chancery Appeals Reports* and *Tennessee Chancery Appeals Decisions* (a collection of the opinions of the Court of Chancery Appeals, in existence from 1895 to 1907),[4] and the *Tennessee Court of Civil Appeals Reports* (containing leading cases from the Court of Civil Appeals from 1909 to 1919). This last reporter is also occasionally referred to as *Higgins Reports*, in honor of the justice who edited and published it.

While virtually all of the Tennessee Supreme Court's opinions are officially published in the *South Western Reporter*, only about ten percent of case opinions from the intermediate appellate courts are officially published. There are two classes of "unofficial" cases in Tennessee: those designated as *not for citation* and those designated as *not for publication*. *Not for citation* cases have no precedential authority and may not be cited in opinions or briefs filed with the court. *Not for publication* cases (which are much more common), may be cited by either courts in their opinions or by litigants in their briefs. They are considered to have persuasive, rather than mandatory, authority.[5] Citing to a published decision, though, is always preferable.

Although these unpublished decisions are not included in the *South Western Reporter*, they may be available from several other sources. Both published and unpublished case opinions starting from the mid to late 1990s (depending on the issuing court) may be found on the web page of the Tennessee Administrative Office of the Courts.[6] Unpublished case opinions are also collected

---

4. Tennessee is one of the few remaining states with a separate set of equity courts, called Chancery courts. Today, appeals from Chancery court go to the Tennessee Court of Appeals rather than to a separate court for chancery appeals.

5. Tenn. Sup. Ct. R. 4(E) and 4(G)(1) (2015). However, this rule is not true in all states. In some states it is not permissible to cite unpublished authority. It is important to know the rule on this issue in the jurisdiction you are writing for.

6. The address is http://www.tsc.state.tn.us/.

and included in Tennessee case law databases on Westlaw, Lexis Advance, and Bloomberg Law. They may also be retrieved using commercial document delivery services. The most popular commercial service for obtaining unpublished case opinions in Tennessee is the *Tennessee Attorneys Memo*, discussed below in this section of the chapter.

Cases from state trial courts in Tennessee are not published; in fact, few states publish opinions at the trial court level. Unpublished opinions may be obtained directly from the court that decided the case, and some are available from online services or the *Tennessee Attorneys Memo*.

Published cases from Tennessee are generally available from the three major legal research database vendors: Westlaw, Lexis Advance, and Bloomberg Law. You can also find them on lower-cost services, including Fastcase (provided free to members of the Tennessee Bar Association) and Casemaker, albeit with fewer editorial enhancements and research aids. While these services include all Tennessee Supreme Court opinions back to 1791, their coverage of intermediate appellate court opinions varies. Tennessee's published opinions are also available for free on Google Scholar, starting from 1950.[7] Some of the older Tennessee intermediate appellate opinions, especially those from more obscure reporters, are only available in print and on some specialized legal databases such as HeinOnline and LLMC Digital.

Additionally, many Tennessee attorneys subscribe to *Tennessee Attorneys Memo* (often called simply TAM), a weekly newsletter that summarizes Tennessee case law, legislation, and other legal news. TAM includes references to both officially published and unpublished cases. TAM subscribers can order the full text of any case opinion from TAM's Case Copy Service, or access opinions through a private online database, TAM Online. TAM also offers options for newsletters and case summaries tailored for specific research interests and practice areas.

B. Reporters and Sources for Federal Court Opinions

1. United States Supreme Court

Decisions of the United States Supreme Court are reported in the *United States Reports*, which is the official reporter; the *Supreme Court Reporter*, which is an unofficial West reporter; and the *United States Supreme Court Reports, Lawyers' Edition*, another unofficial reporter by LexisNexis, frequently referred to simply as "Lawyers' Edition." Although the *United States Reports*

---

7. The address is http://scholar.google.com.

is the official reporter, meaning that you should cite it if possible, that series frequently publishes cases a year or more after they are decided. Thus, for recent cases, you will often cite the *Supreme Court Reporter* or *Lawyers' Edition*. Another source for finding recent cases from the Supreme Court is *United States Law Week*. This service publishes the full text of cases from the Supreme Court and provides summaries of important decisions of state and federal courts.

There are a number of online sources for Supreme Court opinions. The Court's website includes slip opinions soon after the decisions are rendered, sometimes on the same day the decisions are rendered.[8] Google Scholar is another free online resource for finding Supreme Court opinions, and of course they can also be located on Westlaw, Lexis Advance, and Bloomberg Law as well as on Fastcase, Casemaker, and similar lower-priced research services.

2. Lower Federal Courts

Opinions issued by the federal intermediate appellate courts are published in the *Federal Reporter*, now in its third series. The abbreviations for these reporters are F., F.2d, and F.3d. Some Court of Appeals cases that were not selected for publication in the *Federal Reporter* may appear in the reporter series *Federal Appendix*, which West began publishing in 2001. Cases appearing in the *Federal Appendix*, although contained in a print reporter, are still "unpublished." The precedential weight given to unpublished federal appellate decisions varies depending on the jurisdiction, so be sure that you know the rules with respect to citing unpublished opinions before using them in your legal documents.[9]

Selected opinions from the United States District Courts, the federal trial courts, are reported in the *Federal Supplement*, now in its third series. The citation abbreviation for this reporter is F. Supp. Opinions from district courts that interpret and apply federal rules, such as the *Federal Rules of Civil Procedure* or the *Federal Rules of Criminal Procedure*, may be published in the *Federal Rules Decisions* reporter, abbreviated F.R.D.

Published federal opinions are available on Westlaw, Lexis Advance, and Bloomberg Law, together with selected unpublished opinions. They can also

---

8. The address is http://www.supremecourtus.gov.
9. Federal rules permit the citation of unpublished federal cases, but the precedential weight they are assigned varies. Fed. R. App. P. 32.1 & Committee Notes (2012).

be found on Google Scholar from 1923 forward. Unpublished opinions, starting in about 2006, may be accessed through the pay-per-page government website PACER (Public Access to Court Electronic Records)[10] and occasionally directly through the website of the issuing court.

C. Reporters for Other States

Many other states continue to publish their own case reporters, and whether a lawyer cites to a state reporter or to one of the commercial regional reporters from the West National Reporter system will vary depending on the citation rules of the state where that lawyer is practicing. Georgia, for example, publishes its Supreme Court cases in the *Georgia Reports* and decisions of Georgia intermediate appellate courts in the *Georgia Appeals Reports*. Georgia cases are also published in the *South Eastern Reporter*, a counterpart of the *South Western Reporter*. Other regional reporters are the *Atlantic Reporter, North Eastern Reporter, North Western Reporter, Pacific Reporter,* and *Southern Reporter.* Together with its federal reporters discussed above, these comprise the National Reporter system published by West.

Two citations that refer to the same decision in different reporters—for example, citations to the same case in *Georgia Reports* and the *South Eastern Reporter*—are called *parallel citations*. Which reporter to cite to, or whether to cite to both of them, will be governed by a local rule or by a style guide such as the *Bluebook* or *ALWD Guide*. Be aware of which rules govern citation for your particular jurisdiction and the document you are writing.

The coverage of each regional reporter is decided by West, and it does not correspond with the composition of the federal circuits explained in Chapter 1. Because the states were grouped into regions for case-reporting purposes by West in the 1800s, some of the associations can seem counter-intuitive. Most people today would not think of Tennessee as being in the southwest, but Tennessee remains in the *South Western Reporter* because Tennessee was considered to be in the southwest when the reporters were organized. Similarly, cases from Oklahoma can be found in the *Pacific Reporter*, while cases from Nebraska are in the *North Western Reporter*.

II. Editorial Enhancements of a Reported Case

A case decision printed in a reporter contains the exact language of the court's opinion. Additionally, the publisher includes supplemental information

---

intended to aid researchers in learning about the case, locating relevant parts of the case, and finding similar cases. Some of these research aids are gleaned from the court record of the case, while others are written by the publisher's editorial staff. This discussion explains the information and enhancements included in the *South Western Reporter*. Most reporters will include most of these items, though perhaps in a different order. Other reporters published by West will have nearly identical publisher enhancements and information. The case excerpt in Figure 2-1 shows these elements.

Figure 2-1. Example Case from West's *South Western Reporter*

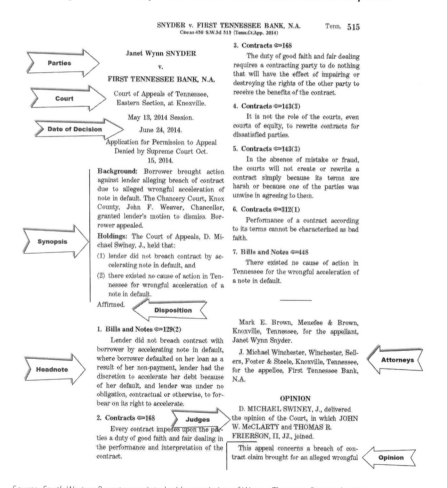

The elements discussed below can also usually be found in the online versions of case opinions, although how they appear and what, exactly, is included may vary depending on the service used. Figure 2-2 shows the same case, *Snyder v. First Tennessee Bank N.A.*, as displayed on Westlaw.

Parties and procedural designations. All of the parties are listed with their procedural designations.[11] In general, a losing party who files an appeal will be called the *appellant* and the opposing party will be called the *appellee*.[12] The traditional form in Tennessee calls for parties in civil cases to be designated by their procedural status both at the trial level and at the appellate level.

Court. Immediately after the listing of parties, the court that decided the case will be listed. In most other states, and in older Tennessee cases, the *docket number* will also be included. The docket number is a record-keeping number assigned to the case by the court and is unique to that case — rather like a Social Security number for a case. While the docket number is no longer included in the official publication of the *South Western Reporter*, you will still see it when researching case law online using a service such as Westlaw, Lexis Advance, or Bloomberg Law.

Dates. Each case will include the date of the court's decision. Some cases may also include the date that the case was argued and submitted to the court, or a date that a higher appellate court denied further review or hearing. For citation purposes, usually only the year that the case was decided is necessary.

Synopsis. One of the most helpful research aids added by the publisher is a synopsis. This is a short summary of the key facts, procedure, legal points, and disposition of the case. Reading a synopsis can quickly tell you whether a case is on point. You cannot rely exclusively on a synopsis; at least skim each case to determine whether it is important for your research. Moreover, you must never cite the synopsis, even when it gives an excellent summary of the case or repeats text from the opinion. The synopsis itself is not authoritative.

Disposition. The disposition of the case is the court's decision to affirm, reverse, remand, or vacate the decision below. If the appellate court agrees with only part of the lower court's opinion, the appellate court may affirm in part and reverse in part.

Headnotes. A headnote is a sentence or short paragraph that summarizes a single point of law in a case. Most cases will have several headnotes. The text

---

11. Recently, Tennessee cases have been reported with the procedural designations of the parties noted only in the *Attorneys* section, discussed below.

12. In other jurisdictions, the term *respondent* is used for the appellee in this situation.

Figure 2-2. Sample Case on Westlaw

of the headnote may come directly from the text of the opinion, or it may be an editor's paraphrase of the text. But because only the opinion itself is authoritative, do not rely on headnotes when analyzing cases, and do not cite them in legal documents. In West reporters, each headnote will have a *topic*, such Animals, and a *key number*, such as 74(8). How to use these topics and key numbers to find additional cases on the same subject is discussed in Section III.A. of this chapter.

Each headnote within a case is assigned a sequential number, i.e., the first headnote is headnote number one, the second headnote is headnote number two, and so on. If you determine that headnote number three in a case you are reading is the most pertinent to your issue, you can skim through the text of the opinion and look for the bold, bracketed[3][13] in the opinion. This number will show you where, in the opinion, the point of law summarized in headnote number three can be found. In an online version of a case with headnotes, the headnote numbers will be hyperlinked so that you can move back and forth between the headnotes and the points of law in the opinion that the headnotes summarize.

Headnotes are the product of a given reporter's editorial staff. Thus, in states where case decisions are published in more than one reporter, the number and text of the headnotes will likely differ depending on which reporter is being used.

Attorneys. The attorneys representing each of the parties, the attorneys' law firms, and the cities in which they practice are listed. In recent Tennessee cases, the listing of the attorneys is also where you will find the parties identified with their procedural designation, such as appellant or plaintiff.

Opinion. The text of the opinion is immediately preceded by the name of the judge who wrote the opinion. In some cases, the names of the judges who heard the opinion may be listed, and those who concurred or dissented will be noted. Note that following a judge's name may be "C.J." or chief justice (for the Tennessee Supreme Court), "P.J." or Presiding Judge (for the Tennessee Court of Appeals or Court of Criminal Appeals) or "J." for another judge or justice. Judges sitting by special designation will be listed as "Special Judge."[14]

If the judges who heard the case do not agree on the outcome or the reasons for the outcome, there may be several opinions for the case. The opinion sup-

---

13. In some reporters, the numbers are printed in bold but not bracketed.
14. For example, a trial judge or retired appellate judge invited to hear an appeal would sit by special designation.

ported by a majority of the judges is the *majority opinion*. An opinion written to agree with the outcome but not the reasoning of the majority is a *concurring opinion*. An opinion written by a judge who disagrees with the outcome supported by the majority opinion is a *dissenting opinion*. While only the majority opinion is binding precedent, the other opinions provide valuable insights and may be cited as persuasive authority. If there is no majority on both the outcome and the reasoning, the case will be decided by whichever opinion garners the most support, which is called a *plurality decision*.[15]

The items included in a case opinion will vary not just from state to state, and publisher to publisher, but also over time. Comparing current Tennessee cases from the *South Western Reporter* with older Tennessee cases from the *South Western Reporter* will reveal significant differences in how cases look and what information is published with them. Additional parts of case opinions that you may see in other reporters include a background section that summarizes the procedural posture of the case, a concise summary of the court's holdings, notation of parallel citations to reporters from other publishers, and library references that give cross-references to the relevant sections of secondary sources, such as legal encyclopedias or treatises.[16]

III. Researching Judicial Opinions

Many factors affect the decision to use print or online case law research. Several of the important factors to consider include the cost of the information, access to online and print resources, amount of time to complete the work, importance of current information, how much information and understanding you have about the subject being researched, and personal preferences. Because most researchers today rely on online research for finding judicial opinions, this chapter will consider them first.

---

15. In Tennessee, as in many states, appellate cases are heard by a three-judge *panel* of the full appellate court. In many other states, a party who does not agree with the decision of the appellate panel may ask for a rehearing *en banc*, meaning that all of the judges on that court would rehear the case. Tennessee, however, does not allow for *en banc* rehearing at the intermediate appellate level, and a party who seeks another hearing must petition the state Supreme Court.

16. A summary of the law in an encyclopedia or treatise could provide valuable background information and refer to additional cases or statutes that are on point.

Table 2-2. Accessing Tennessee Case Law on Research Databases

Bloomberg Law	Court Opinions → State Court Opinions → Tennessee (click names of courts to include in search)
Lexis Advance	Cases → Cases by State → Tennessee (select courts or groups of courts to include in search)
Westlaw	Cases → Cases by State → Tennessee (select courts or groups of courts to include in search)

A. Researching Case Law Online

There are many methods of finding cases online, but following two general rules will make your searches more effective. First, if you know you are looking for judicial opinions and not something else, start by narrowing your search field to cases from the jurisdiction you are researching. If you are looking for Tennessee case law, you can follow the steps in Table 2-2 on the respective services to search only Tennessee case law, rather than doing a universal search that will retrieve anything on your research service that corresponds to your search terms (statutes, newspaper articles, regulations, and so on).

Second, remember to take advantage of options to conduct advanced searches and craft your search terms and parameters carefully, instead of just randomly typing a jumble of words into a search bar. When using Westlaw, a particularly powerful way to research cases is using its "Topic and Key Number" case indexing system for accessing case law by subject.

1. Understanding and Using the West Topic and Key Number System

In order to conduct topic and key number-based research on Westlaw, you need to understand the basics of what this indexing system is and how it works. The topic and key number system used by West starts with West's over 400 standardized legal topics. These topics can range from quite broad—Criminal Law and Torts are two such topics—to rather narrow, such as the Turnpikes and Toll Roads topic. Each topic is broken down, in outline form, into many sub-topics. Each sub-topic is assigned a number, called a "key number." Most topics start with key number one and may proceed through just a few dozen key numbers or several hundred, depending on how broad the topic is and how involved litigation surrounding it is. The aim of the West topic and key number system is to identify each point of law in a case and assign it at least one topic and key number. Once you know the topic and key number associated with the issue you are researching, you can use that topic and key number to find published cases from any jurisdiction addressing that issue. For example, if you are researching the liability of a dog owner when his dog bites someone, you could determine that "Animals 66" is the topic and key number dealing with injuries by animals to people. You could then use "Animals 66" to locate all cases identified by West as addressing that issue.

How does this process of assigning topics and key numbers work? West editors read every published case and identify points of law from each case. The editors write a headnote, a summary paragraph concerning that point of law, for each identified point of law in the case. The West editors standardize the language of the headnote, using common language that is likely to be found in similar cases. This standardized language from the headnotes in the Westlaw database may provide a significant advantage for keyword searches.

Once the headnotes are prepared, the West editors assign a topic and key number to each one. In *Snyder v. First Tennessee Bank N.A.*, the case shown in Figure 2-1, headnote number one is classified as Bills & Notes 129(2). West's topics and key numbers remain consistent across jurisdictions. If you found a case with the topic and key number Bills & Notes 129(2) from North Carolina, you could use that same topic and key number to find cases addressing that point of law in Tennessee, California, or anywhere else in the country.

Figure 2-3 shows the beginning of the outline, with key numbers, for the Robbery topic.[17] Note that, on Westlaw, the term "key numbers" is often used to refer to topics and key numbers together.

a. Starting with Key Numbers

You can take several approaches to search for cases using the key number system on Westlaw.[18] The first is to select the "Key Numbers" link on the opening page. Then either search for key numbers that are relevant to your issue, or

---

17. You can see that the topic Robbery has a separate number associated with it: 342. When the key number system is used online, West also gives each topic a number. While this can be confusing, the number is used simply because computers deal better with numbers than with words. In general, this "topic number" can be safely ignored. Just focus on the name of the topic and the key numbers you have determined are relevant to your research.

18. This system is proprietary to West and is not available on Lexis Advance or Bloomberg Law. Both Lexis Advance and Bloomberg Law do have systems of headnotes and topic classification outlines, but they are not as in-depth and comprehensive as the West system, nor are they as widely used by legal researchers.

Figure 2-3. Westlaw Topic

Source: Westlaw, image reprinted with permission of West, a Thomson Reuters business.

browse through the topic and key number table to find a good starting point. Once you find a key number that appears relevant to your particular issue, you can either browse or search the headnotes for that key number to find on-point cases. If you are researching an issue of Tennessee law, at this point you would use the "Change Jurisdiction" link near the search bar to focus on Tennessee cases. Once you have found your on-point key numbers and selected the jurisdiction you want to search, enter your search terms in the search bar to locate case opinions. Keep in mind that when you do your searching starting from the "Key Numbers" page, you are just searching the content of the headnotes prepared by the West editors, not the full text of the case opinions. So, if you are researching when drug detection dogs may be used to inspect a car during a traffic stop, you could search or browse the Key Numbers page to determine that Automobiles 349 is a relevant key number, as it deals with traffic stops. You could then search for the word *dog* within Automobiles 349, and Westlaw would retrieve all cases from Tennessee that have a headnote classified as Automobiles 349 and that use the word *dog* in that headnote.

Once you have conducted your search, the filters on the left of the results page allow you to refine your results further by searching for additional terms within the headnotes, changing or limiting your jurisdiction, or focusing on a particular date range.

Another way to improve your results is to search either a broader or narrower set of key numbers. Because the key numbers for each topic are arranged according to a hierarchical outline of the law, you can choose to search a broad range of key numbers within a topic (if you are not sure exactly what key number might be associated with relevant cases for your issue) or just one key number. Often, cases relevant to a particular issue may be classified under different, but closely grouped, key numbers, so searching just one key number may mean missing pertinent results.

Figure 2-4. Westlaw Headnote

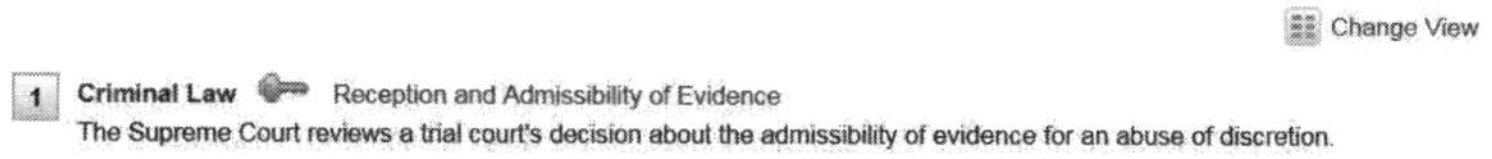

⊞ Change View

1 **Criminal Law** ⚷ Reception and Admissibility of Evidence
The Supreme Court reviews a trial court's decision about the admissibility of evidence for an abuse of discretion.

Source: Westlaw, image reprinted with permission of West, a Thomson Reuters business.

b. Starting with a Retrieved Case on the Screen

Another way to access the digest online is to select a topic and key number from a relevant headnote of a retrieved case on Westlaw. Once you have found a relevant headnote, just click on the description of the issue that comes after the key symbol in order to run a search for more cases assigned to that topic and key number. Figure 2-4 shows a headnote summarizing a point of law in the Criminal Law topic. To find additional cases dealing with this specific key number, click on "Reception and Admissibility of Evidence."

To see more detail about the topic and key number for the headnotes on Westlaw, click the "Change View" link in the upper right of the headnote field. This alternate view will allow you to see the relevant portion of the topic outline, and adjust your searching accordingly. Figure 2-5 shows this more detailed view.

When you are using this more detailed view, you can click on any of the numbers underneath the key symbol in the right column to run a search for more cases associated with that topic and key number. Clicking on the top entry—110—is the broadest search and will retrieve cases associated with the topic Criminal Law. Each entry in the list gets progressively narrower in its scope, so you can adjust your search depending on how specific you want your results to be.

After you run your search using the key number system, you can narrow and focus your results by searching for particular words within your results, limiting your results by date or court, and changing your jurisdiction. You can also switch the order of your results from the default chronological order to

Figure 2-5. Westlaw Headnote: Detailed View

⊞ Change View

1	**Criminal Law**	⚷		
	The Supreme Court reviews a trial court's decision about the admissibility of evidence for an abuse of discretion.	110	Criminal Law	
		110XXIV	Review	
		110XXIV(N)	Discretion of Lower Court	
		110k1153	Reception and Admissibility of Evidence	
		110k1153.1	In general	

Source: Westlaw, image reprinted with permission of West, a Thomson Reuters business.

"most cited," which potentially places the most important and respected cases on this issue at the top of your results.

2. Using Advanced Search Features

Westlaw, Lexis, and Bloomberg Law all offer options for searches that are more sophisticated than just entering search terms that might be found somewhere in the full text of case opinions. On Westlaw, you start by selecting the case law database you wish to search, then click the "Advanced" link just to the right of the universal search bar. This will bring up a search template where you can narrow your search to only particular parts of the text of the case. You can also use the more advanced terms and connectors searching described in Chapter 1.

You might choose to limit your search just to the text of the headnotes. Searching for *contaminat! & food* in the "Headnote" field will bring up every case in your chosen jurisdiction that has any form of the word "contaminate" and the word "food" in the headnotes. This can help focus your search on the cases where food contamination is an important part of the case, rather than just being mentioned somewhere in the opinion in passing. There are several other fields you can search on Westlaw, such as the "Synopsis" field, which searches just the summary of the case prepared by West editors, and the "Words & Phrases" field, which searches for cases that include a judicial definition of a particular word or phrase.

To access advanced searching on Lexis, click on "Cases" under "Content Type" on the main Lexis screen, then click "Advanced Search" just above and to the right of the search box. Lexis's advanced search template allows you to search specific fields such as the case summary, the overview, and the authoring judge. The searchable fields on Bloomberg Law are less extensive than those on Westlaw and Lexis, and are included in the basic search screen for case law. On Bloomberg, you can search by party name, authoring judge, attorney, and for cases associated with a pre-defined topic, but there is no way to specifically search a case summary, synopsis, or headnotes.

3. Using Pre-Selected Subjects

Westlaw, Lexis Advance, and Bloomberg Law all have ways to explore collections of cases that have been pre-selected as being relevant to certain subjects of law. These pre-selected cases can be a good way to access case law as a starting point when you are unfamiliar with an area of law and are not certain of exactly what keywords to use. Table 2-3 shows the steps to access these pre-selected cases in each of the services.

Table 2-3. Finding Case Law in Pre-Selected Subject Areas

Online Research Service	Steps
Bloomberg Law	Practice Centers tab → Choose topic → Opinions & Dockets
Lexis Advance	Browse → Practice Pages → By Practice Area → Choose topic → Primary Sources → Case Law
Westlaw	Practice Areas tab → Choose topic → Cases

B. Researching Case Law in Print: The West Digest System[19]

The West topic and key number system was initially developed for use in print, not online, and for decades, that was the exclusive way that legal researchers accessed the system. This print system, comprising the various West digests and West reporters, still exists, and many researchers continue to prefer using the print version.

As noted above, the West editors read every published case and summarize the points of law in the opinion. These summaries are called headnotes, and each headnote is assigned a topic and key number (or multiple topics and key numbers) from the West topic outline. In both online and print versions of opinions published by West, the headnotes are placed immediately before the text of the opinion. In the print digests, the headnotes are also reprinted—without the case opinions—in the separate books called *digests*. In the digests, the headnotes are organized by topic, and within each topic, by key number. In this way, they function as an index to case law within a particular jurisdiction. So, if you know that Criminal Law 1153 is the relevant key number for the issue you are researching, you can find the digest for your jurisdiction, locate the volume with the topic Criminal Law, and then turn to Criminal Law 1153 to find headnotes from cases in your jurisdiction addressing this point of law.

West publishes digests for specific states, for regions corresponding to some of its regional reporters, and for the federal courts; it also publishes a comprehensive digest addressing all courts. Tennessee researchers focused on state law would typically use *West's Tennessee Digest 2d*. There is no regional digest encompassing Tennessee. Other digests you may come across and find useful include the *Federal Practice Digest* (for federal cases) and the *Decennial Digest*,

---

19. This part of the chapter draws from *North Carolina Legal Research* and is used with permission.

which allows research on opinions from courts across the country. Just as with the online version, the topics and key numbers remain consistent across jurisdictions.

There are several ways to access the West Digest system in print. Which one you use will depend on how much information you have as a starting point, as well as the complexity of your issue and your level of familiarity with the digests.

1. The "One Good Case" Method

Occasionally, you will begin a project with a known, relevant case in hand. For example, a more experienced attorney may suggest that you look at the *Martinez* case from several years ago because she thinks it might be relevant. You could then find the *Martinez* case and note the topic and key number associated with the most relevant of its headnotes, for example, Witnesses 337.[20] Find the digest volume with the Witnesses topic, then look up the key number 337 within that topic. There you will find headnotes from all the cases addressing that legal issue in that jurisdiction. This is perhaps the easiest way of using the digest.

2. The Descriptive-Word Index Method

Typically, however, you won't be starting with a case already in hand. Rather, your starting point will simply be a legal issue or question. In that situation, the best starting point will likely be the "Descriptive-Word Index." The purpose of the Descriptive-Word Index is to help you find topics and key numbers that match up with the issue you are researching. Once you find relevant key numbers in the Descriptive-Word Index, look them up in the main digest volumes to locate headnotes from relevant cases. The steps compiled in Table 2-4 outline the process for using the Descriptive-Word Index.

Table 2-4. Process for Searching with Descriptive-Word Index

Step 1	Generate search terms using TARPP or another method.
Step 2	Search for the terms in the Descriptive-Word Index. Note all relevant topics and key numbers. Remember that you must have both a topic and a key number to look up. The topics in the Descriptive-Word

---

20. In many instances, a relevant case will have multiple headnotes with different topics and key numbers that are germane to your research, so this would be a multi-step process.

Index are abbreviated. If you have trouble deciphering an abbreviation, check the list of topics in the front of the volume.

Step 3   Update your index research by looking in the pocket part to the Descriptive-Word Index.

Step 4   Look up your topics and key numbers in the main digest volumes.

Step 5   Update your research by checking for additional headnotes in the pocket parts to the main digest volumes, in supplements, in reporter and advance sheet digests, and online.

a. Generate Search Terms

The first step is to generate a list of search terms. Chapter 1 addressed this task and suggested using a brainstorming technique such as the TARPP (things, actions, remedies, people, and places), or the journalistic approach of who, what, how, why, when, and where. Of course, the more specific and relevant your search terms, the easier it will be to connect with relevant topics and key numbers in the digest.

b. Search for Terms in the Descriptive-Word Index

The second step is to search the Descriptive-Word Index and note all relevant topics and key numbers. The index is arranged alphabetically. Look up each search term in the index and record the topics and key numbers that you find. Keep looking up your search terms in the index until you have finished with all of them: do not be tempted to take the first relevant topic and key number you find and go directly to looking it up in the main digest volumes.

During this process, you may note patterns emerging, such as most of the findings falling under one or a small number of topics in the index, or perhaps most of the findings falling within a small area of key numbers of a larger topic. These are all good signs, but they are not always present. Some research issues are spread across a number of topics. Don't be discouraged if the index suggests relevant cases in a number of topics rather than being confined to one or two.

Sometimes novice researchers are frustrated at their inability to identify search terms that match up with terms in the Descriptive-Word Index. A combination of factors could be causing that outcome and there are several alternatives. Rethink the search terms and consider any additional search terms describing the legal issue.

c. Update Index Findings by Using the Index Pocket Parts

The third step is to check the pocket part in the back of the Descriptive-Word Index for any new references added since the hardbound volume was

last published. Each volume of the index is only republished after there is sufficient new information to warrant the expense. So each year, in the intervening
time, new information is published in a pocket part and placed in the back of
each volume. The pocket part will contain all the new information since the
volume was last published. It is important to check the pocket part for each
volume of the digest that is used throughout this process.

d. Look Up Your Topics and Key Numbers in the Main Digest Volumes

The fourth step is to move from the Descriptive-Word Index to the main
volumes of the digest to check the specific topics and key numbers identified
from the Descriptive-Word Index. The topics are printed on the spine of the
volumes and are arranged throughout the digest set in alphabetical order. Select
the topic volume and find the key number in the topic you are researching.
Several smaller topics might all be contained in one volume, while some larger
topics may span multiple volumes of the digest.

After locating the topic, quickly browse the information at the beginning
of the topic that describes the legal subjects covered by that topic. Another
section, "Subjects Excluded and Covered by Other Topics," might also be useful.
Under the topic heading is a table of contents of all the key numbers for that
topic, referred to as "Analysis" or "Topic Analysis." If a topic has many key
numbers, you might first see a summary analysis and then the more detailed
analysis that includes all the key numbers. You will usually benefit from browsing the analysis to see where the key numbers you identified from the index
fit within the larger framework of the topic.

Look at each of the key numbers identified from the Descriptive-Word Index
and read the case headnotes. Record the case name and citation to any case
that appears relevant and worth reading based upon review of the headnote.
Although this process takes time, it is critically important to the outcome of
the research. Careful and thorough review of the key numbers and headnotes
will provide more certainty when conclusions are drawn and decisions are
made at the end of the research project.

Although you might be researching a legal issue with a particular outcome
in mind, you must read the headnotes and related cases objectively and not
fear cases that suggest an unfavorable outcome. Be certain that the opposing
attorney will find and use these cases; they are certainly cases that you need
to identify and address in the research and lawyering process. For example,
can a case that is "bad" for a particular viewpoint be distinguished? If not,
would the client have an alternative legal theory? This is part of the art of
practicing law.

e. Update Your Digest Research

The fifth step in the case research process using digests is to update the information from the topic volume. To begin updating, check the volume's pocket part for the same topics and key numbers. Occasionally, a pocket part becomes too large to fit within the binding in the back of a volume. West then publishes the pocket part information as a free-standing paperback supplement, usually shelved adjacent to the main hardbound topic volume.

After publication of the annual pocket parts, as the year progresses and new cases are decided, the digest might add a cumulative supplementary pamphlet. These pamphlets are usually shelved at the end of the digest set and should be checked, if available, to continue updating.

All of these types of supplemental materials will have a table indicating the extent of their coverage, called a "closing table." If you are researching in *West's Tennessee Digest 2d*, the most recent supplementary pamphlet may have a closing table with an entry that reads "Closing with Cases Reported in South Western Reporter, Third Series: 452 S.W. 3d 80." This information in the closing table is important, especially if you are going to continue updating in print: if so, make a note of this entry and move on to the final step.

The final step in updating is to locate any additional cases for your topic and key number that were published after the last supplement for the print digest. The easiest way to do this is to go on to Westlaw, access the key number system online, and retrieve all cases from your jurisdiction assigned to the key number you are researching. You can filter by date so that you only retrieve cases issued after the date of the last supplemental pamphlet that you checked.

Without access to Westlaw, you can take steps to bring your researching even more up to date than just checking the print supplements housed with the digest itself. The closing table has told you the volume and page number of the reporter containing the last case included in the cumulative supplementary pamphlet. In the example above, that was volume 452, page 80 of the *South Western Reporter 3d*. You are going to take this information and use the reporter series to work forward, checking each reporter volume and issue published after volume 452, page 80. Each reporter volume of any West reporter set, such as *South Western Reporter*, includes a miniature digest of the cases included in the volume. Find the reporter volume (452 *South Western Reporter 3d*) identified by the cumulative supplementary pamphlet and look up your topic and key numbers in that individual volume's digest to find any relevant cases in that volume. Do this for each subsequent volume and advance sheet for that reporter. This process will ultimately bring you up to approximately several weeks from the present time. To be more current beyond the most recent reporter advance sheets, you must go online.

3. Topic Analysis or Outline Method

After researching a legal issue numerous times, you should become familiar with both the language associated with issue and the language used by the digest to describe and identify the issue. Also, using the digest over time develops an understanding of how to effectively use it. When you have gained either or both of these experiences, you may want to try the "Topic Analysis Method" or "Outline Approach." These approaches involve selecting the appropriate topic volume from the shelf (bypassing the Descriptive-Word Index) and examining the Topic Analysis or Outline and finding relevant key numbers.

The danger with this method is that you might entirely miss non-intuitive topics that have relevant key numbers. The Descriptive-Word Index is designed to prevent that from happening; however, if an attorney practices criminal law for example, and has practiced for some time using the digest to find case law, she might be in a position to work directly from the "Criminal Law" topic.

4. Words and Phrases Method

Opinions containing judicial definitions of a word or phrase may be found using the "Words and Phrases" volumes of the digest. Obviously, a judicially defined word or phrase is useful for a common law legal subject where there are no applicable statutory definitions. A judicial definition of a term is superior to a generic legal dictionary definition since the judicial definition is more specific to the relevant jurisdiction. Also, judicially defined terms are useful when interpreting statutory law that may include vague terms or terms not defined in the statute. The Words and Phrases volumes, which are typically shelved near the Descriptive-Word Index volumes, are arranged alphabetically by word, just like a dictionary. After finding the applicable Words and Phrases volume, you just look up your term alphabetically to find headnotes including the definition. Another useful feature of a "Words and Phrases" entry is the list of the relevant topics and key numbers used for headnotes in the case that defined the term.

C. Other Methods of Finding Cases

Online searching and using the West digest system are hardly your only options for finding relevant case law. Other methods are discussed throughout this book, including using annotated codes (Chapter 3), citator services (Chapter 6), and secondary authorities such as treatises and law reviews (Chapter 7). Whenever you are faced with finding case opinions on a particular topic, make sure you consider all possible methods and select the one best suited to the issue you are researching and the sources you have available to you.

IV. Reading and Analyzing Case Opinions[21]

Once you locate a case, you must read it, understand it, and analyze its potential relevance to the problem you are researching. Do not expect reading a case opinion to be easy. It is perfectly normal for beginning lawyers to read complex decisions at around ten pages per hour. Often this reading is interrupted by looking up unfamiliar words and concepts. Early efforts will be more productive if you have a basic understanding of civil procedure terms and the fundamental aspects of case analysis, then follow the strategies outlined at the end of this chapter.

A. A Thimbleful of Civil Procedure

Civil litigation begins when the *plaintiff*—the person who believes he or she was harmed—files a complaint against the *defendant*.[22] The *complaint* names the parties to the lawsuit, states the facts giving rise to it, references applicable law, and asks for relief. Courts vary considerably in how much information is required at this stage of litigation. In general, the complaint must be at least specific enough to put the defendant on notice of the legal concerns at issue and to allow her to prepare a defense.

The defendant has a limited amount of time in which to file a response to this complaint. In Tennessee, the defendant must file a response within thirty days of being served with the complaint.[23] If the defendant does nothing within the prescribed time, the plaintiff can ask the court for a *default judgment*, which would grant the plaintiff the relief sought in the complaint. The most common form of response to the complaint is an *answer*. In the answer, the defendant admits to the parts of the complaint that she knows are true, denies

---

21. This part of the chapter draws from *Oregon Legal Research* and is used with permission.

22. In certain actions, such as those arising out of estate administration or in the context of family law, the party initiating the action may be called the *petitioner* and the party who the suit is against is called the *respondent*.

23. Tenn. R. Civ. P. 12.01.

those things she disputes, and asserts no knowledge of other allegations. The defendant will also raise any available affirmative defenses.

Throughout the litigation, parties submit a variety of documents and briefs to the court for its consideration. Some require no action or response from the court, for example, the filing of the complaint. In other instances, a party asks the court to make a decision or take action. An example is a motion for summary judgment, where a party asks the court to decide in that party's favor without the need for a trial.

When the trial judge grants a motion that ends a case, the losing party can appeal. The appealing party is called the *appellant,* and the opposing party is the *appellee.*[24] In deciding an appeal from an order granting a motion, the appellate court decides whether the trial judge was correct in issuing the order at that stage of the litigation. If the appellate court finds that the trial judge made no error, it will *affirm.* If not, it will *reverse* the order granting the motion and *remand* the case back to the trial court.

Even at trial, the parties may make motions that can be appealed. For example, during the trial, the plaintiff presents his evidence first. After all of the plaintiff's witnesses have testified, but before the defendant's witnesses are called, the defendant may move for *judgment as a matter of law,* arguing that the plaintiff cannot win based on the evidence presented, and asking for an immediate decision. An order granting that motion could be appealed.

Many reported case decisions are appeals of orders granting motions. These cases apply different standards of review, depending on the motion that is the subject of the appeal. While standards of review are beyond the scope of this book, understanding the procedural posture of the case is crucial to understanding the court's holding. For example, an opinion of an appellate court could hold that the facts submitted in a defendant's motion for summary judgment in a products liability case did not merit granting a summary judgment, and reverse the trial court. This opinion would have little relevance in another products liability case, no matter how factually similar, if the second case has been tried by a jury and a verdict rendered, because the two cases are in different postures and different standards will apply. The relevant rules of civil procedure will guide your analysis. Texts listed in Appendix B of this book contain helpful explanations as well.

---

24. In many other jurisdictions, "appellant" and "appellee" are used at the intermediate appellate level, while the highest court uses "petitioner" and "respondent" to refer to the parties.

B. Analyzing the Substance of Case Opinions

Early in your career it may be difficult to determine whether a case is relevant to your research problem. If the case concerns the same legally significant facts as your client's situation and the court applies law on point for your problem, then the case is relevant. Legally significant facts are those that affect the court's decision. Some attorneys call these "outcome-determinative facts" or "key facts." Which facts are legally significant depends on the case. The height of the defendant in a contract dispute is unlikely to be legally significant, but that fact may be critical in a criminal case where the only eyewitness testified that the thief was about five feet tall.

Rarely will your research reveal a case with facts that are exactly the same as your client's situation. Rather, several cases may involve facts that are similar to your client's situation, but not exactly the same. Your job is to determine whether the facts are similar enough for a court to apply the law in the same way and reach the same outcome. If a court reached a decision favorable to your client, you will highlight the similarities. If, on the other hand, the court reached an unfavorable decision from your client's perspective, you may argue that the case is distinguishable from yours based on its facts or that its reasoning is faulty.[25] You have an ethical duty to ensure that the court knows about a case directly on point, even if the outcome of that case is adverse to your client.

You are also unlikely to find one case that addresses all aspects of your client's situation. Most legal claims have several elements or factors. *Elements* are required parts of a claim while *factors* are important aspects but not necessarily required. For example, in many jurisdictions, the elements of a claim for battery are the following:

- The defendant committed an intentional act that resulted in a harmful or offensive contact with the plaintiff;
- The plaintiff did not consent to the contact; and
- The harmful or offensive contact caused injury, damage, loss, or harm to the plaintiff.

---

25. This discussion assumes that you are preparing a pleading to file in court in which you advocate on behalf of your client. While preparing in-office memoranda, it is important to remain as even-handed as possible in your description and analysis of applicable authorities, so that the client and other attorneys working on the case can make the best judgments possible as to likely case outcomes and the best way to proceed.

If a court decides that one of these three elements is not met, it often will not discuss the others, as without all three required elements present, the case will fail.

In a different type of case, a court may look at a list of factors rather than elements. In most jurisdictions, in a negligence case, a court will look at certain factors to determine whether the defendant has taken an unreasonable risk. These factors include the following:

- The foreseeable probability of the harm or injury occurring;
- The possible magnitude of potential harm or injury;
- The importance or social value of the activity engaged in by the defendant;
- The feasibility of alternative, safer conduct and the relative costs and burdens associated with that conduct; and
- The relative safety of the alternative conduct.[26]

The court may decide that two factors are so overwhelming that others have little impact on the outcome, and thus address those other factors only briefly, if at all. In these circumstances, if the other factors or elements were important to your case, you would have to find additional cases that analyze them.

Once you determine that a case is relevant to some portion of your analysis, you must decide how heavily it will weigh in your analysis. Two important points need to be considered here. One is the concept of binding precedent; the other is the difference between the holding of the case and dicta within that case.

A case opinion that has decided an issue or principle of law is *binding precedent* with respect to later cases presenting the same issues to lower courts in the same jurisdiction.[27] Thus, the courts must follow prior opinions of higher courts in the same jurisdiction, ensuring consistency in the application of the law. When deciding state law issues, the Tennessee Court of Appeals must follow the decisions of the Tennessee Supreme Court, but not those of the courts of any other state, not the decisions of lower courts in Tennessee, not the decisions of any federal court, and not even earlier decisions of the Tennessee Court of Appeals.

The concept of binding precedent is related to the doctrine of *stare decisis,* which means to "stand by things decided."[28] Under the doctrine of *stare decisis,*

---

26. *See McCall v. Wilder,* 913 S.W.2d 150, 153 (Tenn. 1995) (citing Restatement (Second) of Torts, §§ 292, 293 (1964)).

27. *See Black's Law Dictionary* 1366 (Bryan A. Garner ed., 10th ed. 2014).

28. *Id.* at 1626.

courts generally follow their own previous decisions instead of re-opening an issue for a possible different outcome. If a court decides not to continue following its earlier opinions, it is usually because of changes in society that have outdated the law of the earlier case or because a new statute has been enacted that changes the legal landscape.

Courts are required to follow only the holdings of prior cases, that is, the courts' ultimate decisions on the matters of law at issue in the cases. Other statements or observations included in the opinion are not binding; they are referred to as *dicta*. For example, a court in a property dispute may hold that the land belongs to X. In reaching that decision, the court may note that had the facts been slightly different, it would have decided the land belonged to Y. That observation is not binding on future courts, though it may be cited as persuasive authority.

Finally, in determining whether an earlier decision is binding precedent for your issue, you must determine whether that earlier decision has been reversed, overruled, or modified in a way that substantially affects the holding in question. To do this, legal researchers use citator services such as Shepard's and KeyCite. Citator services are discussed in depth in Chapter 6.

After finding a number of cases that have similar facts, that discuss the same legal issue, and that are binding on the court that would hear your client's case, the next step is to synthesize the cases in order to state and explain the legal rule. Sometimes a court states the rule fully; if it does not, piece together the information from the relevant cases to state the rule completely but concisely. Then use the analysis and facts of various cases to explain the law, decide how the rule applies to the client's facts, and determine your conclusion. Note that this method of synthesis is much more than mere summaries of all the various cases. Legal analysis texts in Appendix B of this book explain synthesis in detail.

C. Strategies for Reading Case Opinions

As you begin reading opinions, the following strategies may help you understand them more quickly and more thoroughly.

✓ Quickly review the synopsis (and summary of holdings, if available) to determine whether the case seems to be on point. If so, skim the headnotes to find the particular portion of the opinion that is most relevant. Remember that one opinion may discuss several issues of law, only one or two of which may interest you. Go to the portion of the opinion identified by the relevant headnote and decide whether it is important for your project.

✓ If so, skim the entire decision to get a feeling for what happened and why, focusing on the portion of the opinion identified by the relevant headnote.

✓ Read the opinion slowly and carefully, giving extra scrutiny to those parts of the opinion that are most plainly relevant to your legal issue.

✓ At the end of each paragraph or page, consider what you have read. If you cannot summarize it, try reading the material again.

✓ The next time you read the case, take notes. The notes may be in the form of a formal case brief or they may be scribbles that only you can understand. Regardless of the form, the process of taking notes will help you identify, parse through, and comprehend the essential concepts of the case. In law school, the notes will record your understanding of the case both for class discussion and for the end of the semester when you begin to review for exams. When preparing to write a legal document, the notes will assist you in organizing your analysis into an outline.

✓ Note that skimming text online or highlighting a printed page is usually not sufficient to achieve thorough comprehension of judicial opinions.

Chapter 3

Constitutions, Statutes, and Procedural and Ethical Rules

I. Constitutions

A *constitution* is the fundamental governing document of a state. It spells out the rights, duties, and powers of the various branches of government, and typically cannot be amended by the legislature alone.

A. The Tennessee Constitution

The first Tennessee constitution was adopted in 1796. This constitution, largely modeled on the constitution of neighboring North Carolina, was in many ways remarkably democratic, and was described by Thomas Jefferson as "the least imperfect and most republican of the state constitutions."[1] It allowed the vote to all free men over the age of twenty-one, regardless of race or property ownership. The governor was to be directly elected, rather than selected by the legislature. Voting, in a striking change from practices followed elsewhere, was to be conducted by secret ballot.

However, there were problems with the first constitution. One of the primary criticisms was that the legislature was given too much power, and the governor, too little. A constitutional convention was called in 1834, and a new constitution was ratified in 1835. The major changes emerging with the new constitution included strengthening the executive and judicial branches, changes to taxation, and, in a major step backwards, reserving the power to vote to white men only. The full text of the Constitutions of 1796 and 1835 are set out in an appendix at the end of Volume 1 of the *Tennessee Code Annotated*.

---

1. Lewis Laska, *The Tennessee State Constitution: A Reference Guide*, pp. 4–6 (1990) (quoting Ramsey, *The Annals of Tennessee to the End of the Eighteenth Century*).

After the Civil War and following four years of state government controlled by Union sympathizers, a constitutional convention was held in 1870. A new constitution was ratified in 1870, and the Constitution of 1870 remains the basis for the current constitution. Most of the changes to the constitution adopted in 1870 were made in response to what were seen as excesses and corrupt practices by Governor William ("Parson") Brownlow and the Unionist government. The right of suffrage was expanded, and the powers of the governor greatly diminished.[2]

The Tennessee Constitution has been amended several times since 1870. Some of the changes were brought about via constitutional conventions (in 1953, 1959, 1965, 1972, and 1977), and others via a legislation-and-referendum method. These amendments dealt with issues as weighty as school segregation and as seemingly trivial as the term of office for trustees.

In many respects, the provisions of the Tennessee Constitution parallel those of the United States Constitution. Article I of Tennessee's constitution ensures religious liberty, freedom of the press, the right to a jury trial, and the right to be free from unreasonable searches and seizures. Articles II through VII delineate the powers of the various branches and departments of government. However, like many other state constitutions, the Tennessee Constitution also covers some matters often thought of as being more statutory in nature. For example, Article II, Section 33 prohibits the issuance of state bonds to railroads that are in default in paying interest on earlier state bonds.

B. Researching the Tennessee Constitution

The Tennessee Constitution is published, together with annotations, in the first volume of the *Tennessee Code Annotated*, immediately following the United States Constitution.[3] A separate index to the Tennessee Constitution is included in the back of Volume 1 of the *Tennessee Code Annotated*. This set also has a multi-volume general index, shelved at the end of the set, providing references to both state and federal constitutions and to statutes.

---

2. In the aftermath of the Civil War, the right to vote had been stripped from Confederate sympathizers. The 1870 Constitutional Convention restored the vote to the former rebels and their allies. The Constitution of 1870 also severely limited the power of the governor to use the state militia. Laska, *The Tennessee State Constitution*, pp. 14-16. Governor Brownlow had used the state militia to attempt to halt the predations of the newly formed Ku Klux Klan.

3. It is also published in the first two volumes of *West's Tennessee Code Annotated*, an unofficial publication of Tennessee's statutes and constitution.

The Tennessee Constitution is also available online with the same useful annotations. The two publishers of the *Tennessee Code Annotated*, the official publisher LexisNexis and also West, provide the same information online at their websites, Lexis Advance and Westlaw. Bloomberg Law also provides the text of the current Tennessee Constitution in its Tennessee Legislative database, but that database lacks annotations similar to the Lexis and West versions.

In addition to availability on these "premium" sources, the Tennessee Constitution is also available online from lower cost or free legal information websites. For example, the official publisher of the *Tennessee Code Annotated*, LexisNexis, provides free access to the Tennessee Constitution[4] but this version also lacks the premium annotations found in the Westlaw and Lexis Advance versions. Also, even though LexisNexis is the official publisher of the Code, this free digital version is not official.

The Tennessee General Assembly provides a link to a free, annually updated, PDF version of the Tennessee Constitution prepared by the Office of the Chief Clerk of the Senate.[5]

Whichever version or format of the constitution you select, begin constitutional research by generating a list of research terms from the facts and issues of your problem, as explained in Chapter 1. Search the indexes for terms and record the references given. For example, the general index contains under the term "Searches and Seizures" references to Article I, Section 7 of the Tennessee Constitution and also references to related statutes.

If possible, once you find a provision of the Tennessee Constitution that applies to your problem, check the annotations that follow immediately after it. Cases that have interpreted that part of the constitution will be summarized and cited. If there are numerous cases that have discussed a particular section, their summaries will be organized by topic, with a table of contents provided at the beginning. The annotations may also provide historical notes and citations to law review articles, treatises, and opinions of the Tennessee Attorney General, all of which may be helpful in learning about a particular constitutional provision. If using a print version from one of the annotated codes, be sure to check any recent pocket parts or free-standing supplements for the most recent amendments to the constitution as well as new cases and interpretative materials. If using a digital version of the constitution, be sure to note the date

---

4. The free, unannotated version of the constitution provided by LexisNexis is available at https://www.lexisnexis.com/hottopics/tncode.

5. The constitution is available in PDF from the Tennessee General Assembly at http://www.capitol.tn.gov/legislation/publications/index.html.

of the version you are using and confirm that no changes have been made since that date.

Resources available for researching Tennessee constitutional conventions will vary depending on the convention. More recent constitutional conventions, such as those of 1977 and 1965, were recorded in detail, and all of the debates and documents were published in indexed, bound volumes, such as the *Journal of the Debates of the Constitutional Convention of the State of Tennessee* (1977). Earlier conventions were not as well documented, but journals and papers do exist. The *Journal of the Proceedings of the Convention of Delegates Elected by the People of Tennessee* documents the 1870 constitutional convention, while the *State of Tennessee Constitutional Convention of 1959*, of course, records that of 1959. However, access to these documents may be limited.

Other possible sources to find journals and proceedings for early Tennessee constitutional conventions include microfiche sets such as CIS's *State Constitutional Conventions* or paid subscription databases such as *The Making of Modern Law*. Check with a librarian at your library for access to such services. Additionally, well researched, newer articles may be available online that address specific issues addressed at the conventions. For example, see "The Two 'Great Issues' of the Constitutional Convention of 1870," by Sam Elliott in the *Tennessee Bar Journal* and available from the Tennessee Bar Association website for lawyers and students with membership access.[6]

C. Researching the Federal Constitution

The United States Constitution is published as part of the sets the *United States Code*, the *United States Code Service*, and the *United States Code Annotated*, which are discussed in more detail in Part II of this chapter. While the version of the U.S. Constitution published in the official *United States Code* is poorly annotated, the versions in the *United States Code Service* and *United States Code Annotated* are heavily annotated by useful cases and secondary sources interpreting the Constitution. Free versions of the U.S. Constitution are available from a number of sources. Additionally, the federal government publishes "The Constitution of the United States of America—Analysis and

---

6. The address of the article on the bar's website is http://www.tba.org/journal/the-two-great-issues-of-the-constitutional-convention-of-1870. Otherwise, find the article at *Tennessee Bar Journal*; May 2015, Vol. 51 Issue 5, p20.

Interpretation"[7] which is updated periodically and aids in understanding and interpreting the Constitution.

Just as with researching the Tennessee Constitution, whether using a print or digital version, the first step is usually to find an index to the constitution. Using your search terms to locate relevant provisions, read these applicable sections and determine how they apply to your legal issue. An annotated version of the U.S. Constitution will include relevant judicial decisions and secondary sources that will assist in interpreting and applying the constitution.

II. Statutes

Statutes could affect almost every legal issue you deal with in practice. Many new researchers are surprised to find that statutes, rather than cases, will be the primary focus of much or even most of their professional research and analysis, given the common law system's well-known high regard for case law.[8]

Statutes may address substantive issues, such as whether someone who serves alcohol to another who is obviously already drunk can be held liable for any injuries that result from an accident involving the drunk individual. Statutes can also affect related, procedural issues, such as a statute of limitations, which sets the amount of time a potential litigant has to file a lawsuit. Areas of law that have developed more recently, such as the use of electronic signatures, or software licensing, will typically be governed by statutes.

A. Publication of Statutes

When a law is first enacted, it is published in an individual format called a *slip law.* The name "slip law" derives from the traditional publication of statutes on individual slips of paper, rather than being bound into a book with other statutes. Most states have done away almost entirely with distribution of slip laws in paper and now publish them only in electronic format. Tennessee is

---

7. This publication is browsable from the main FDsys website, https://www.gpo.gov/fdsys. The FDsys website is scheduled to be replaced by https://govinfo.gov/ in 2017. See Chapter 5 for more information.

8. Because law students, especially early in their law school careers, spend tremendous amounts of time and energy focused on reading and interpreting case opinions, they particularly receive an impression that judicial authorities are what they will spend the vast majority of their professional lives researching.

one of those states.[9] Researchers looking for recent Tennessee legislation will find it online at the Secretary of State's website.[10] The acts are indexed by legislative session and browsable as well as searchable by keyword.

Most Acts passed by the Tennessee General Assembly are Public Acts and are generally applicable. Like most legislatures, however, the General Assembly also passes Private Acts that only have local effect.

After the conclusion of each legislative session, all the laws passed in that session are published in the *Public and Private Acts of the State of Tennessee,* which is also referred to as the "Tennessee session laws." *Session laws* is a generic term for a series in which all the laws passed by a legislature in a legislative session are published, with the laws arranged chronologically.

The laws passed by the legislature and signed by the governor are then *codified,* meaning that they are integrated into the *Tennessee Code Annotated,* which contains all laws currently in effect in Tennessee, arranged by subject. The *Tennessee Code Annotated* is divided into seventy-one *titles,* each on a particular subject. For example, Title 36 contains domestic relations laws, and Title 68 consists of laws on health, safety, and the environment. Each title is further subdivided into *chapters* that address particular topics in each subject area, and each chapter is broken down into individual *sections.* Within Title 36, Chapter 1 deals with adoption, and Section 119 of that chapter addresses the filing of a final order of adoption. A citation to that particular law reads: Tenn. Code Ann.§ 36-1-119.

There are two versions of the *Tennessee Code Annotated* currently published in print and online. The official print version is published by LexisNexis, and it should be the version to which you cite if at all possible.[11] The Lexis-Nexis version is available on Lexis Advance. West publishes an unofficial version of the *Tennessee Code Annotated* both in print and online in Westlaw. The text of the statutes themselves, as well as their arrangement and numbering, will be the same in each set of publications. Both the LexisNexis and West versions are extremely well annotated with relevant cases interpreting the statute and secondary authorities explaining relevant legal issues. These editorial enhancements added by the publisher will vary between the two publishers.

---

9. Tenn. Code. Ann. § 12-6-116 (2011).

10. The address is http://sos.tn.gov/division-publications/acts-and-resolutions .

11. While LexisNexis's online *Tennessee Code Annotated* on Lexis Advance corresponds with its print version, you should cite to the official print version rather than the online version.

Bloomberg Law also maintains a database of the current Tennessee code. However, it is not annotated like the LexisNexis or West versions. To browse or search it, follow this path from the Search & Browse tab on the main webpage: select State Law, then select Tennessee from the interactive map, and choose the Tennessee Legislative link.

A free, unannotated version of the code is also available from LexisNexis, entitled the *Tennessee Code Unannotated*.[12] While the text of the actual code language should be identical to the official version by the same publisher, the free version is not official. Additionally, the lack of case law and secondary authority annotations in the code are severe limitations to the overall research process.

B. Researching Statutes in the *Tennessee Code Annotated*

There are a number of different approaches to finding statutes that bear on a research issue. Table 3-1 outlines the basic process. The most efficient approach will vary depending on the issue you are researching and the other resources you have available. It is important to be flexible in your research and recognize that, if one approach is not working, you may want to rethink your strategy and try a slightly different method. Whichever method you choose, make sure that you start with an expansive list of research terms by brainstorming using the journalistic or TARPP method from Chapter 1.

As mentioned in Chapter 1, often an excellent initial step in your research process is to use secondary authorities. Particularly when you are new to an area of law, a secondary authority such as a practitioner's manual can explain the law and put it in context while also providing citations to the controlling statutes. Keep in mind that you would never simply rely on someone else's interpretation of the law, even if that person wrote the most prestigious and well respected treatise on the subject. You will always want to read the underlying primary authorities, including statutes, for yourself, and make your own conclusions about how they affect your legal research issue.

Table 3-1. Outline for Tennessee Statutory Research

1.   Generate a comprehensive list of search terms.

2.   Look up those search terms in the index to the *Tennessee Code Annotated* to find references to relevant statutes. Alternatively, browse the tables of

---

12. The address for the free version is http://www.lexisnexis.com/hottopics/tncode/.

contents in the relevant code titles, read pertinent secondary sources to find citations to the statutory code, or use the search terms to search an online database of the *Tennessee Code Annotated.*

3.   Locate, read, and analyze the potentially relevant statutes in the *Tennessee Code Annotated.*

4.   Refer to the annotations following the text of any relevant statutes to find citations to related statutes, cases that interpret the statutes, and additional explanatory materials.

5.   Read and analyze the materials found in Step 4.

1. Initial Print Research Strategy for Statutes

The research process for statutory law, as outlined in Table 3-1, is surprisingly similar regardless of whether you are using print or online codes. The differences concern some of the initial strategies and will be treated separately in this section and the following section 2 below. Section 3 discusses how the research process continues after you've identified relevant statutes, regardless of whether you are using print or online format.

a. Using a Citation or Popular Name

If you are fortunate enough to begin your research with a statutory citation already in hand, simply look up the code section in a print code. The citation Tenn. Code Ann. § 39-14-404, for example, means the statute will be found in Title 39, chapter 14, section 404. Look for the volume that contains Title 39, then page through that volume until you find chapter 14, and then section 404.

Occasionally, you may have the popular name of a session law, such as the Skills for Jobs Act. If so, you can find the act in the Popular Name Table in the index volume of the code.[13] The entry will provide basic information about the act describing where the act is codified.

b. Browsing the Index for Search Terms

Without a statutory citation or the popular name of a session law, you must have relevant search terms to use in searching the Code. See Chapter 1 for a discussion of the journalistic approach or the TARPP method of developing search terms.

---

13. The West version of the *Tennessee Code Annotated* contains a Popular Names Table, but the Lexis version does not.

With search terms in hand, use the latest index volumes to find citations to relevant code sections. A good index should contain all important terms within the code. Additionally, the index should include related relevant terms with "see" or "see also" references for those logical terms with which researchers are likely to approach the index, but that don't actually appear in the text. In that way, the index is a superior method of connecting the researcher's search terms with related subjects in the code compared to online keyword searching.

c. Browsing the Table of Contents for Relevant Chapter Names

An alternative approach, if you have some understanding of your research topic, is to browse the Table of Contents of the code. In Tennessee, this means browsing the seventy-one titles to select the most relevant title. Each title of the *Tennessee Code Annotated* has a table of contents, as does each chapter within each title. The danger associated with this method is that statutes are sometimes not where you might imagine them to be, or related statutes may spread across several titles. For example, if you are trying to find the statutes related to the crime of driving under the influence of alcohol and spend your time skimming through the tables of contents for Title 39, Criminal Offenses, you will miss the relevant statutes in Title 55, Motor Vehicles. The more information you have about the subject of law being researched and the structure of the code, the more likely this approach will be successful.

d. Updating Print Code Books

When researching using code books, make sure to check whether the statute has been amended or repealed. Hardbound code books are initially kept current with a softbound pocket part tucked into the back cover of the volume. Pocket parts are published annually. Hardbound code volumes may also be kept current with freestanding softbound supplements that are shelved either next to each hardbound volume, or at the end of the code set. Recent amendments to a law, and information indicating whether a law has been repealed, will be found in these supplemental volumes if a hardbound volume is more than a year old. The new materials in these volumes are organized by statute number, so it is easy to look up a statute and note any changes. If you do not find any reference to the statute in the supplemental materials, the statute was not amended or repealed during the time between publication of the hardbound volume and the supplemental volume or pocket part.

Since pocket parts are published only annually, there is always a chance that, if the legislature is in session, your law has been amended or repealed and that fact has not yet been noted in a pocket part or free-standing supplement. The next step in finding the current print statutory materials should be to look at the end of the entire *Tennessee Code Annotated* set for softbound "Advance Legislative Service" books, which will include tables showing how the most recently passed legislation affects the current code.

Finally, the last step in updating a statutory law section is to go online using a citator service, such as Shepard's on Lexis Advance or KeyCite on Westlaw, to get the most recent updates.[14] If these are not available, you might access the Tennessee General Assembly website as an alternative to search for any recently passed legislation that might have affected the statute.

After finding and updating the relevant statute using *print* resources, skip the next section (section 2) and see the following section 3, "Continued Research Strategy Regardless of Format," for a discussion of how to proceed.

2. Initial Online Research Strategy

Strategies for researching your issues in online versions of the code are similar but bear some explanation.

a. Using a Citation or Popular Name

If you are starting your statutory research with a citation, simply select the Tennessee Code Annotated database in the online system and enter the citation in the main search bar to retrieve the section.

To begin searching with the popular name of a session law that is now codified, such as the Skills for Jobs Act, enter the popular name as a phrase in the Tennessee Code Annotated database in Westlaw, Lexis Advance, Bloomberg Law, or the free Tennessee Code Unannotated website. Alternatively, find the act in the Popular Name Table—an alphabetical listing of popular statute names with citations and hyperlinks to the corresponding statutory code sections—available from the Tennessee Code Annotated database search screen on Westlaw.[15]

b. Browsing the Index of the Code Online

Westlaw and Lexis Advance allow you to browse the index of Tennessee Code Annotated online. This approach combines the convenience of online access with the value of a human-mediated index. Rather than retrieving only

---

14. Using online citator services to *update* your research is discussed more fully in Chapter 6.

15. The other services do not provide a Popular Names Table.

results that match your exact search terms from a keyword search, a search of the index will include terms that are not necessarily in the text of the statutes you are searching, but that are logical terms associated with it that a keyword search would not retrieve. This provides a greater opportunity to find relevant documents. To access the index on Westlaw, go to the main search screen for the Tennessee Code Annotated, then look for the "Tennessee Statutes Index" link in the "Tools & Resources" column on the right side of the page. On Lexis Advance, type *Tennessee code index* into the universal search bar in order to either search or browse the index. The online versions of the Tennessee Code provided by Bloomberg Law and for free do not offer indexes.

c. Searching the Code by Keyword

As with all full-text keyword searching where you will be searching every word in every document in the database, the best practice is to search the smallest database you believe will have all of the relevant documents. If possible, you might narrow your keyword search to the specific chapters of the code you believe will have relevant sections. The danger of this approach is that you might miss relevant sections hidden in unlikely chapters of the code. However, a comprehensive research process, such as the process discussed in this book, will decrease the chances of missing any relevant law.

After selecting the smallest database, develop a well designed search taking advantage of advanced search options. These include phrase searching as well as searching fields in Westlaw or segments in Lexis Advance.

Note that, although the Bloomberg Law search engine employs terms and connectors search operators, the system lacks the sophistication and search alternatives provided by Westlaw and Lexis Advance. Even less sophistication is available in the search engine for the free Tennessee Code Unannotated website.

In addition, the lack of annotations in the codes in Bloomberg Law and at the free website negatively affects efficient searching. In the databases on Westlaw and Lexis Advance, the annotations are searched along with the text of the code. The case summaries and other annotations provide additional words related to your subject beyond the text of the statute to which your search terms will be exposed. This feature may enhance the quality of your retrieved results. In those rare instances when searching the text alone (without the annotations) is more efficient, the Bloomberg Law website and the free website are good choices. You might also choose to use the advanced search options on Westlaw or Lexis Advance to limit your keyword searching to the text of the statutes alone, omitting searching the annotations.

d. Browsing Chapters as a Table of Contents

After developing some understanding of the legal subject being researched and the structure of the code, you might successfully browse the code's chapters as a table of contents to locate the relevant statutory law. This feature is available online at Westlaw, Lexis Advance, Bloomberg Law, and the free website.

3. Continued Research Strategy Regardless of Format

Once you have found a potentially relevant statute, whether using print statutory codes or researching online, follow the research strategy below. This strategy will help you understand the statute and apply it to the facts.

a. Read Statutory Law

Reading statutory language is not like any other legal reading task. Unlike a judicial decision written by a single judge or with the input of a small number of judges, statutory law is created in a legislative process involving large numbers of people, often with different perspectives. Statutory language may be difficult to interpret for a number of reasons. Perhaps language in a statute is intentionally vague for the purpose of achieving the largest number of supporters and therefore being acceptable to the widest range of viewpoints. Alternatively, perhaps the legislative intent was to be as specific as possible, but the language is simply open to various interpretations. Reading the statute several times is often a common necessity to understand its provisions and identify any uncertainty.

Several strategies assist researchers in understanding statutes. Both relate to the concept of context. The first strategy is to look for statutory definitions. Statutory definitions may be different from our everyday definitions of words. Go up the hierarchy from the relevant code section to the subchapter, chapter, or even title to look for applicable definitions. Reading any definitions might clarify statutory meaning. A second strategy is to take a few minutes and read the individual statute in the context of the surrounding sections and even the entire part or subchapter. Consider how your section fits into the larger scheme. The added context of the whole might assist you in understanding the meaning of an individual section.

For an example from the *Tennessee Code Annotated*, examine the statute in Figure 3-1. Tenn. Code Ann. §39-14-404 concerns "especially aggravated burglary." To understand the statute, the researcher has to refer to another section, 39-14-402, which provides the definition of burglary, as well as to 39-14-401, which defines terms such as habitation. Section 40-35-111 provides the penalty for committing a Class B Felony.

Figure 3-1. Example Tennessee Statute

Tenn. Code Ann. § 39-14-404. Especially aggravated burglary. —

(a) Especially aggravated burglary is:

    (1) Burglary of a habitation or building other than a habitation; and

    (2) Where the victim suffers serious bodily injury.

(b) For the purpose of this section, "victim" means any person lawfully on the premises.

(c) Especially aggravated burglary is a Class B felony.

(d) Acts which constitute an offense under this section may be prosecuted under this section or any other applicable section, but not both.

[Acts 1989, ch. 591, § 1; 1990, ch. 1030, § 24.]

---

b. Find and Read Cases Interpreting the Statute

No matter how carefully you read and understand the meaning of a statute, you must review any judicial decisions that may have interpreted the statute. If a judge in your jurisdiction has interpreted a code section, that interpretation must be used, reinterpreted, or challenged. If a judicial interpretation exists, it cannot be ignored. The Notes of Decisions or Case Notes at the end of each code section are summaries of cases and the relevant law applicable to the statute. The summaries include a citation to the full text so that you can find and read any relevant authorities. When using the print version, this process also includes examining the pocket part and any supplementary pamphlets issued as part of the code. After reviewing all of the relevant case summaries, locate and read each of the relevant cases summarized in the Notes of Decisions or Case Notes since the summaries are not legal authority, but simply an editor's interpretation.

c. Interpret and Apply the Statute to the Facts

The court's primary task in interpreting a statute is to ensure that the legislative purpose or intent is achieved. This task may be accomplished, in the absence of any special definitions in the code, first by examining the statute and according to the language its plain and ordinary meaning.

> The duty of [the court] in construing statutes is to effectuate legislative
> intent. Legislative intent is to be ascertained primarily from the natural

and ordinary meaning of the language used. Where the language used
is devoid of ambiguity, [the court] must apply its plain meaning without a forced interpretation that would limit or expand the statute's
scope.[16]

If the plain and ordinary meaning of the language of the statute does not
lead to a reasonable interpretation, the courts in Tennessee have relied on additional guidance. The meaning of the statute may next be determined by its
legislative history and the circumstances around the creation of the law suggesting what problem was intended to be addressed by the legislation.[17] See
Chapter 4 for a discussion of researching Tennessee legislative history. Another
approach to the interpretation of a vague statute is the application of the rules
or maxims of statutory construction.[18]

d. Understanding Statutory History

Yet another tool in the interpretation of a statute is the understanding of a
statute's history.[19] After the text of each statute, you will find the *statutory
history line* (also called *statutory credits*), which tells when the statute was enacted, amended, and repealed. That line also provides citations to the session
laws with the text of those acts that enacted, amended, or repealed the statute.
Generally, the substantive law that will apply to a situation is the law that was
in effect when the events happened. Thus, you must always check the statutory
history line to be sure that the statute was in effect and has not been amended
since the events you are researching took place. As an example, if you are researching the law on homicide with respect to a homicide that took place five
years ago, you need to be sure that the law on homicide has not been amended
in the intervening five years. If the homicide law had been amended in the intervening five years, you would have to research in archived code materials
and the session laws to find the applicable version of the statutes.

Figure 3-1 shows the statutory history line for Tenn. Code Ann. §39-14-
404, Especially Aggravated Burglary, in the last line: Acts 1989, ch. 591, §1;

---

16. *Kyle v. Williams*, 98 S.W.3d 661 (Tenn. 2003) (citations omitted).
17. *Shore v. Maple Lane Farms, LLC*, 411 S.W.3d 405 (Tenn. 2013); *see also Chapman
v. Sullivan County*, 608 S.W.2d 580 (Tenn. 1980).
18. An analysis of this approach is beyond the scope of this book. For more discussion, see Norman J. Singer, *Statutes and Statutory Construction* (7th ed., West Group
2007), also known as *Sutherland Statutory Construction*. *See also* "Codified Cannons
and the Common Law of Interpretation," 98 Georgetown L.J. 341 (2010).
19. A full discussion of researching legislative history is presented in Chapter 4.

1990, ch. 1030, §24. This statutory history line tells the researcher that the law was first passed in 1989, and the text of the original law can be found in the *Public and Private Acts of the State of Tennessee* for the year 1989, in Chapter 591, Section 1. The law was then amended in 1990, and the text of the amendment can be found in the *Public and Private Acts of the State of Tennessee* for 1990, in Chapter 1030, Section 24. Almost always, in statutory history lines, the punctuation that separates one reference to a session law from the next is a semi-colon. The first session law that appears in a statutory history line is a reference to the initial enactment of a law. The following references will be in chronological order and will refer to amendments, re-numberings, or repeal of the law.

e. Additional Tennessee Code Annotated *Tables, Annotations, and Aids*

In addition to annotations to important case opinions, the *Tennessee Code Annotated* contains annotations and references to additional sources. These annotations appear after each statute. Tennessee Attorney General opinions that interpret the statute and comments from administrative or legislative bodies involved in drafting the statute may be referenced. There are also cross-references to related statutes and references to secondary authorities, such as practitioner's manuals and law review articles, that discuss the statute. These references provide a helpful starting point for further research.

Volume 13 of the code set is the Tables volume, which allows researchers to translate former statute numbers to current statute numbers, and vice-versa. Several times in Tennessee history, the entire set of state statutes has been completely re-numbered. Thus, a case opinion from the 1950s will contain citations to statutes that bear little or no relation to the current statutory numbering scheme. To find the current statute that relates to the statute cited in the 1950s, use the Tables volume to look up the old citation and find a reference to the current statute. The Tables volume also includes mortality, annuity, and valuation tables that are referenced in the Code. In addition, a chart of Tennessee counties and municipalities showing where to find their charters in the *Tennessee Code Annotated* or the *Public and Private Acts of the State of Tennessee*.

The last two volumes of the *Tennessee Code Annotated* contain procedural rules and rules of evidence. Both are important for lawyers practicing in Tennessee courts, as explained below in Part III.

C. Researching Statutes of Other States

Most state jurisdictions codify their statutory law in a similar manner to the method used in Tennessee. Several states, such as New York and Texas, publish their statutory law in volumes by subject name ("New York Penal Law Code") rather than by an overall numbering scheme ("Title 39"). But otherwise, the research strategies discussed in this chapter would apply directly in those and other states as well.

Westlaw, Lexis Advance, and Bloomberg Law provide convenient, if expensive, online access to all fifty states' codes. Also, some academic law libraries still collect print versions of some states' codes. Like Tennessee, many states also provide an unofficial, unannotated version of their state's code freely available on the Internet. Most states' free statutory code may be retrieved using Google or another search engine. There are also some "mega" websites with convenient links to free legal information that might organize access to free state statutory codes. Such sites include Justia[20] and Cornell's Legal Information Institute.[21]

D. Researching Federal Statutes

Federal statutes are researched in much the same fashion as state statutes. Laws that are enacted by the United States Congress are known as *public laws.* They are first printed as slip laws, which are simply individually published acts of Congress. Eventually, slip laws are published at the end of the legislative session in *Statutes at Large,* which serves the same session law publication function as the *Public and Private Acts of the State of Tennessee.* Next, the new statutes are codified and incorporated into the federal statutory code, the *United States Code,* where they are arranged by subject.

Public laws are freely available almost immediately upon adoption at Congress.gov,[22] a government-supported website for federal legislative information. Public laws are also quickly available on the Westlaw and Lexis Advance websites. In the research process, public laws serve as a snapshot of a statute as it was originally passed by Congress. Beyond the historical importance, public laws serve little research purpose. A statutory law researcher usually wants the most currently updated version of the statute and needs to see the statute in the context of the other related statutes concerning that subject. Therefore, rather than using *Statutes at Large* or public laws online for general statutory research, the researcher will most often use one of the versions of the United States Code.

---

20. The address for Justia is http://www.justia.com.
21. The address for the Cornell Legal Information Institute is http://www.law.cornell.edu.
22. The address for Congress.gov is https://www.congress.gov.

1. United States Code

The *United States Code* (USC) is the official federal statutory code, published by the government, arranged by subject. It comprises fifty-three titles. The USC is published every six years. In the intervening years, an annual one-volume supplement is published. Typically, the supplements are several years out of date by the time they are published. Most practitioners cannot rely on information this old. The USC is not annotated with related secondary sources and important case summaries explaining how the statute has been interpreted. Fortunately, several privately published versions of the United States Code are updated more often and have many additional benefits discussed below. Therefore, the official USC has limited usefulness in the research process, as most researchers turn to one of the privately published annotated codes. Many courts, however, still require documents submitted to them to cite the official USC.

The United States Code is freely available digitally from several government websites. The Government Publishing Office's Federal Digital System website[23] provides a link to the Code archived back to 1994.[24] The USC from the Government Publishing Office shares the same weaknesses as the official printed version. It is no more current than the print version and lacks annotations. The USC is also available from the Legal Information Institute.[25] It too shares the same weaknesses. However, the United States House of Representatives Office of the Law Revision Counsel (LRC), the organization that codifies the new statutory law as it is passed by Congress, provides a free online code that is up to date within several days of new laws being enacted.[26] There are also privately published versions of the code, described below, that have editorial enhancements and may be even more up-to-date.

2. *United States Code Annotated* and *United States Code Service*

West publishes the *United States Code Annotated* (USCA). Although unofficial, the text of the USCA should be identical to the official *United States Code*. The USCA, available in print or on Westlaw, is annotated with extensive summaries of cases interpreting the statutes and citations to the cases where they can be read. Other annotations include secondary authorities such as relevant legal encyclopedia articles, ALR annotations, and the appropriate topics

---

23. The address is https://www.gpo.gov/fdsys.

24. The Government Publishing Office is currently beta testing a new website that will replace FDsys. See https://www.govinfo.gov for information.

25. The address is www.law.cornell.edu/uscode.

26. This version of the code is found at http://uscode.house.gov.

and key numbers from the West Digest System, which can be important in the research process. For example, after finding the relevant statute, the researcher can use the case summaries to identify relevant cases interpreting the statute and use the included citations to find and read the cases. Also, the associated topics and key numbers can be used to find relevant cases in all jurisdictions through the West Digest System either in print or on Westlaw.

LexisNexis Publishing produces the *United States Code Service* (USCS), which is another unofficial annotated code. This code, available in print or on Lexis Advance, excels at providing summaries of the most important cases (as opposed to near comprehensive coverage attempted by West in the *United States Code Annotated*). USCS also offers the best coverage of administrative law through annotated citations.

Because of the many annotations and editorial enhancements made by West and LexisNexis, the USCA and USCS will not be found online for free; they are only available on Westlaw and Lexis Advance, respectively.

3. United States Code on Bloomberg Law

Bloomberg provides a United States Code database that is currently updated but lacks the annotations provided by *United States Code Annotated* or *United States Code Service*. However, Bloomberg has created a case law search mechanism that allows a researcher to select a "case analysis" link to execute a search for relevant cases on the spot. This serves as a method of locating relevant case law to assist in the interpretation of each code section.

4. General Research Strategies for the Unites States Code

Because the *United States Code* is structured in a similar manner as the *Tennessee Code Annotated*, the same research methods are appropriately applied. A detailed analysis of researching the federal code is beyond the scope of this book; however, a review of the previous sections regarding researching, updating, and using the print and online versions of the *Tennessee Code Annotated* will provide excellent instruction for this purpose.

III. Court and Ethical Rules

Court and ethical rules are frequently published in, or as companions to, statutory codifications. Court rules govern litigation practice from the filing of initial pleadings through the conclusion of the final appeal. Rules dictate procedural requirements ranging from the correct caption for pleadings to the standard for summary judgment. Court rules like the Tennessee Rules of Civil Procedure and the Tennessee Supreme Court Rules are primary authority even when the court or legislature responsible for them has delegated rule-making power to a council, committee, or other body. Success in litigation may depend as much on compliance with these rules as on the merits of the claim.

A. Tennessee Court Rules

As noted above, the *Tennessee Code Annotated* includes separate volumes that contain the Tennessee Rules of Civil Procedure, the Tennessee Rules of Criminal Procedure, and other procedural rules for various court systems in Tennessee. These rules are available in other sources as well. A compilation of rules is often referred to as a *deskbook*. West publishes a set of deskbooks for each state. The West deskbook for Tennessee is the *Tennessee Court Rules*. This particular set has three volumes. The first contains Tennessee federal court rules, for example, *Local Rules of the United States District Court for the Eastern District of Tennessee*. The second volume contains Tennessee state court rules, such as the *Tennessee Rules of Evidence*. The third volume contains local rules, such as the *Sixth Judicial District Local Rules of Practice (Knox County)*. For some states, the West deskbook set has only one or two volumes, for federal and state court rules, and omits the third volume of local rules.

Some rules are available online. The website of the Tennessee Administrative Office of the Courts, provides a "Court Rules" link with links to most of the statewide court rules sets, some local (county-wide) rules, as well as proposed new rules and amendments.[27] Tennessee rules are also available on Lexis Advance and Westlaw.

Rules are written in outline form like statutes, and they should be read like statutes. Read each word carefully, refer to cross-referenced rules, and scan other rules nearby to see if they are related. After finding a rule on point, look for cases that apply it. Usually the first step in looking for cases that apply a rule is to locate an annotated version of the rule, which will include summaries of, and citations to, case opinions. The rules published as part of the *Tennessee Code Annotated* are, as the name indicates, annotated with references to related cases. The West deskbook set, *Tennessee Court Rules*, is not annotated. You may also be able to find related case opinions by looking in the *Tennessee Digest* or in practitioner's manuals or other secondary authorities. Never assume that

---

27. The address is http://www.tncourts.gov/courts/rules.

a Tennessee rule precisely mirrors its federal counterpart, or that cases applying a federal rule will be relevant to the application of a Tennessee rule.

The text of some rules is accompanied by commentary from the committee charged with drafting or amending the rules. The commentary is persuasive authority.

Be sure that you are working with the current rule. West's deskbooks are published yearly, so they are reasonably current. The court rules volumes published with the *Tennessee Code Annotated* are also published yearly. Usually the first source to publish the most recent court rules and amendments is the website of the Tennessee Administrative Office of the Courts. The newsletter *Tennessee Attorneys Memo* may also include the text of important new court rules and amendments.

B. Federal Court Rules

Similar rules exist at the federal level. They are published in *Tennessee Rules of Court: Federal* as well as in USC, USCA, and USCS. Placement of the rules within each of these publications varies. Sometimes the rules are integrated with the volumes of statutes for Title 28; other times the rules are in separate volumes at the end of the entire code. Each federal circuit and district court may have its own local rules with specific practices required by that court. Local rules for Tennessee's federal courts are found in the volume *Tennessee Rules of Court: Federal.* This volume contains local rules for the Sixth Circuit and for all the federal district courts and bankruptcy courts in Tennessee.

Other sources of federal court rules include a looseleaf series, *Federal Local Court Rules*, which compiles all federal local court rules from across the country and is a helpful source if you have access to it. Also, most federal local court rules are freely available on the Internet.[28] The rules can also be found in Westlaw, Lexis Advance, and Bloomberg Law.

Cases relevant to federal court rules can be found using the annotations of the rules in USCA and USCS, or by referring to the *Federal Practice Digest*, the *Federal Rules Service*, and the *Federal Rules of Evidence Service*. There are also in-depth treatises on federal procedure and rules that provide extensive citations to cases interpreting and applying federal rules.[29]

---

28. One online source is the US Courts website, http://www.uscourts.gov/court-locator.

29. For example, James Wm. Moore et al., *Moore's Federal Practice* (3d ed. 1997) and Charles A. Wright & Arthur R. Miller, *Federal Practice and Procedure* (2005).

C. Professional Rules

The conduct of lawyers in Tennessee is regulated by the Rules of Professional Conduct, which are found in Rule 8 of the *Tennessee Supreme Court Rules*. The chapters of the Rules of Professional Conduct are set out in Figure 3-2.

Figure 3-2. Chapters of the *Rules of Professional Conduct*

---

1. The Client-Lawyer Relationship

2. The Lawyer as Counselor, Intermediary, and Dispute Resolution Neutral

3. Advocate

4. Transactions with Persons Other Than Clients

5. Law Firms, Legal Departments, and Legal Service Organizations

6. Public Service

7. Information About Legal Services

8. Maintaining the Integrity of the Profession

The version of the Rules of Professional Conduct found in the *Tennessee Code Annotated* is, in fact, annotated, and includes references to related Formal Ethics Opinions of the Tennessee Board of Professional Responsibility, judicial opinions, and law review articles. This is the best source for an annotated version of the rules. These rules can also be found in the West deskbook *Tennessee Rules of Court: State*, and on the internet at the Tennessee Administrative Office of the Courts site.[30]

Like most other jurisdictions, Tennessee adopted these new rules using the American Bar Association's *Model Rules of Professional Conduct* as a blueprint. The new rules were originally proposed by the Tennessee Bar Association, and the drafts of the proposed new rules were the subject of much study and debate. The rules and many of the reports and comments regarding the new rules are available on the Tennessee Bar Association's website.[31]

Because Tennessee adopted a new ethical code in 2003, some of the references may be opinions and articles written with respect to the prior ethical code. While the former and current codes share some similarities and language, authorities that interpreted and enforced the old code will be considered persuasive as to the new code rather than mandatory. Also, because Tennessee's *Rules of Professional Conduct* are based on the ABA's *Model Rules of Professional Conduct*,

---

30. The address is http://www.tncourts.gov/rules/supreme-court/8.

31. The address is http://www.tba.org/info/tennessee-rules-of-professional-conduct.

opinions from other jurisdictions interpreting those rules adopted by Tennessee may be considered helpful persuasive authority, particularly if a Tennessee court or the Tennessee Board of Professional Responsibility has not spoken on the issue. You may wish to consult an annotated version of the ABA's *Model Rules of Professional Conduct* in order to find references to decisions from other jurisdictions.

Chapter 4

Researching Legislative History

Chapter 3 largely discussed researching statutory law once codified. This chapter provides a summary of the process by which statutory law is created in Tennessee. An understanding of the legislative process will assist you in finding the legislative documentation produced in making statutory law as well as interpreting the meaning of that law.

Next, armed with an understanding of the Tennessee legislative process, the chapter discusses *tracking* of current legislation as it proceeds through the legislative process. The steps involved in finding the current details of a bill or the status of a bill in the legislature will be described. This knowledge is useful for legal researchers seeking the most current information about proposed or coming changes to statutory law important to their practice.

A more complex task involves using your understanding of the legislative process to gather a complete *legislative history* for a particular statute. Legislative history research is particularly important when trying to determine the meaning of a vague or ambiguous statute. Researching the legislative history of a statute is typically among the most difficult state research tasks to accomplish. States traditionally produce little documentation of the legislative process compared to the federal government. The documentation has also traditionally been difficult to access. The State of Tennessee is no exception. Fortunately, the development of online resources has greatly improved access to the documentation produced in the legislative process in states across the country.

Although there are similarities between the Tennessee legislative process and the legislative process of the United States Congress, the differences are sufficient to warrant separate treatment of the U.S. process at the end of this chapter.

I. Introduction to the Tennessee Legislative Process

Like most states, Tennessee's legislature is prescribed by the state's constitution. Tennessee has a bicameral legislature, known as the General Assembly, composed of two chambers, the House of Representatives and the Senate. The House is composed of ninety-nine members elected for two-year terms each even-numbered year. The Senate is composed of thirty-three members elected for four-year terms. These terms, however, are staggered so that approximately half of the Senators are running for office every two years. Each chamber does much of its work in committees made up of legislators. Each chamber is also supported in its legislative work by a staff of non-legislators who assist with the process.

Each General Assembly convenes for a two-year session beginning in January of each odd-numbered year. Within this framework, the General Assembly typically meets for regular sessions each year from January through May.

A. How a Bill Becomes a Law in Tennessee

An idea for legislation is suggested by a citizen, group, or legislator. A legislator sponsors the bill, and either drafts the language of the bill or has the General Assembly's Office of Legal Services draft the bill.[1] The bill text is important; if enacted, the bill's requirements or prohibitions may affect a client's interests. Even if a modified version is passed, which is likely, comparing the original to the final version can help determine the legislature's intent.

The bill is introduced in either the House or Senate. The Tennessee Constitution requires that bills be considered and passed three times before becoming law. Typically, a bill is introduced and considered for the first time on the same day. If passed, it will be held for second consideration on the next legislative day. After being considered and passed a second time, the Speaker will refer the bill to a legislative committee for hearings or other action. The current bills that are introduced can be found at the General Assembly website under the "Legislation" link where they can be browsed or searched by keyword.[2] Bills from previous sessions can be found archived under the same Legislation link back to the 99th Session beginning in 1995. Bills from 2010 and earlier are also available in print.

---

1. The Tennessee General Assembly, Office of Legal Services offers an excellent Legislative Drafting Guide providing suggestions, recommendations, and best practices for drafting bills. http://www.capitol.tn.gov/joint/staff/legal/2015 Drafting Guide.pdf.
2. They can be found at http://www.capitol.tn.gov.

After a bill has been referred to committee, it will remain there (a result commonly known as "dying in committee") unless one of several courses of action is followed to bring it out.[3] The committee may hold public hearings on the bill. Since the late 1980s, the Tennessee State Library and Archives has been recording hearings held by the standing committees of the General Assembly. For the past several years, committee meetings have also been webcast and the resulting videos archived.

The bill may be passed by the committee, passed with recommended amendments, or rejected or may otherwise die in committee. If the bill is passed, it goes back to the scheduling committee of either the House (the House Committee on Calendar and Rules) or the Senate (the Senate Calendar Committee). The House committee has the power to determine whether a bill will ever be scheduled for third consideration, while the Senate committee is prescribed to schedule every bill referred to it for a vote on the floor of the full Senate. In 1955, the Tennessee State Library and Archives began audio recording the floor sessions of the Tennessee General Assembly. Audio tapes of floor proceedings are available from the Tennessee State Library and Archives, although the recordings are not transcribed.[4] For the past several years, videos of General Assembly sessions have also been webcast, and archives are available online, indexed by bill. Passed amendments and votes are available in the bill history portion of the General Assembly's Legislation page. They are eventually available in the journals of the House and Senate. Current schedules and calendars can be found at the General Assembly website.[5]

When a bill is passed by one chamber, it becomes an *engrossed bill*. The engrossed bill is then presented to the other chamber for consideration. The bill that is passed by both houses is the *enrolled bill*.

Typically, identical bills are introduced simultaneously in both houses. These bills are called "companion bills." If the two companion bills have been amended so that they differ from each other, a conference committee may be appointed to attempt to reconcile the bills. Eventually, both houses must pass identical versions of the bill in order for it to be sent to the Governor.

---

3. For a detailed explanation of those courses of action, see Tennessee General Assembly Legislative Information Services, *How a Bill Becomes a Law*, http://www.capitol.tn.gov/about/billtolaw.html.

4. For more information about Tennessee's recordings of legislative activities, see http://sos.tn.gov/products/tsla/legislative-history-recording.

5. http://wapp.capitol.tn.gov/apps/schedule.

If the Governor signs the bill, it becomes law. If the Governor does not sign the bill within ten days, it becomes law without signature. If the Governor vetoes the bill, the legislature may override with a simple majority vote in both houses.

An enacted bill is assigned a session law number by the Secretary of State's Office; in Tennessee this is called a *public chapter number*. This is a chronological number based on when the bill was passed in that session of the legislature. Session laws (public chapters) are published almost immediately on the Tennessee legislature's website.[6]

Public chapter abstracts and references are available in numerical order every six months based on effective date. Tennessee's session laws are no longer published in print, only online.

The law is *codified*, meaning that it is assigned a number that places it in the code with other laws on similar topics. At the end of each year, the General Assembly passes a *codification bill*, reenacting the general acts of a permanent nature that were enacted by the General Assembly in the preceding year. The annual codification bill integrates recent public acts into the Tennessee Code to make that code, in its updated form, the official compilation of the laws of this state.

Tennessee statutes are officially codified in the *Tennessee Code Annotated* (available in print and on Lexis Advance), unofficially codified in *West's Tennessee Code Annotated* (available in print and Westlaw), and freely available online in an unannotated, unofficial form.[7]

II. Tracking Current Tennessee Legislation

Researchers commonly need to locate current information about legislation pending in the General Assembly. An attorney, for example, may be following a relevant subject related to her practice generally, or perhaps following information relevant to a pending case or client's interest. The process of locating information concerning the status of bills is generically referred to as *bill tracking*. In this process, the researcher typically finds various versions of a bill and learns of the latest activity concerning the bill in the legislative process. There are several sources of bill tracking information.

---

6. The address is http://www.capitol.tn.gov/legislation/publications/index.html.

7. The free, unofficial version of the code can be found at http://www.lexisnexis.com/hottopics/tncode/.

Figure 4-1. Bill Report for House Bill 0114/Public Chapter 127

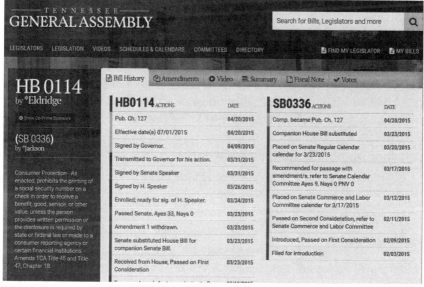

Source: http://wapp.capitol.tn.gov/apps/BillInfo/Default.aspx?BillNumber=HB0114

A. The General Assembly Website

The General Assembly has an excellent website where an enormous amount of current bill information may easily be found.[8]

1. Tracking by Bill Number

The easiest way to track a bill from the current General Assembly session is to use the bill number. From the General Assembly webpage,[9] select "Bill Search" under the "Legislation" link and enter the bill number in the search box. In addition to the various versions of the bill, the retrieved results include the current status of the bill, the bill's sponsors, the vote history of the bill, and a running record of all the activity that has occurred concerning the bill since it was first introduced. The information is usually updated within a day or two during the legislative session. Bill reports, with bill tracking information, are available for bills beginning with the 1995 General Assembly session. See Figure 4-1 for an example of a bill report for House Bill 0114, which went on to become Public Chapter 127, "Social Security Number Disclosure."

---

8. The address is: http://www.capitol.tn.gov/legislation/.
9. The address is http://www.capitol.tn.gov.

2. Tracking a Bill Using "My Bills"

"My Bills" is a free, personalized bill tracking service of the General Assembly that allows you to create up to three lists of bills to track with an unlimited number of bills on each list. My Bills is updated daily. You may log in and view the current legislative status of your bills and see any significant current action on each bill. Alternatively, you can get an RSS feed of major action for your bills, such as when it passes in committee or when it's adopted. The list will last through the end of the biennial legislative session.

3. Other Tracking Options on the Website

Alternatively, perform a keyword search for current bills from the same "Bill Search" box described above. Also, you may browse current bills using an index on the General Assembly website.

These same bill search options, searching by bill number, keyword, or index, are available for previous General Assembly sessions by selecting "Archived" under the "Legislation" link. The archived bill coverage begins in 1995 with the 99th General Assembly.

The result retrieved is a set of bills that will provide the same detailed current status information about bills described above.

B. Other Online Sources for Tracking Tennessee Legislation

Although the freely accessible General Assembly website generally provides the most convenient and current tools for bill tracking, several other sources for bill tracking information exist.

1. Westlaw

Westlaw contains databases for Tennessee bills (current as well as archived back to 2005) and Tennessee bill tracking (also current and archived back to 2005). Note that the free Tennessee General Assembly website's coverage extends back to 1995.

2. Lexis Advance

Lexis Advance contains several databases containing Tennessee bills and bill tracking data. From the Lexis Advance main search page, select "Statutes and Legislation" from the "Content Type" tab, then "Tennessee." From this page, you may select several relevant databases. "TN Full-Text Bills" provides coverage back to 1995. "TN Bill Tracking Reports" covers bill activity back to 1989.

While the "Tennessee Legislative Bill History" database may link to additional information beyond the bill text, the coverage begins in 2006 with gaps in 2008. Because LexisNexis is the official publisher of the Tennessee Annotated Code, the "Tennessee Advance Legislative Service" database provides coverage of legislative additions to the code back to 1989.

3. Bloomberg Law

Public and private acts since 1999 are covered by Bloomberg Law. These can be accessed through the "State Law" link on the main page, then clicking on Tennessee in the United States map, then "Tennessee Legislative."

III. Researching Tennessee Legislative History

A. Why Research Legislative History?

Statutory law is often designed to be generally applicable to a wide variety of circumstances, for example, to prevent a wrong or describe a mandatory way of accomplishing a particular outcome. A relevant statute, once located, must be interpreted and applied in each research situation. Sometimes the language and meaning of the statute is clear. Sometimes, however, the meaning or applicability of the statute may be difficult to interpret. This may be due to the nature of the legislative process, which often requires compromise in the selection of specific words in order to achieve a consensus in the legislature to enact the statute. Another reason why statutory language may be difficult to interpret and apply is that the situation in which the statute is being applied may not have been contemplated by the legislators when they drafted the language of the statute.

The rule on statutory interpretation in Tennessee was best stated by the Tennessee Supreme Court in the 1996 case *Worley v. Weigel's, Inc.*, 919 S.W.2d 589 (Tenn 1996). The Tennessee Supreme Court reviewed statements made by the sponsor of a law during its enactment process in the legislature in order to determine how the statute should be applied to the litigants in the case.[10]

---

10. *See Worley*, 919 S.W.2d at 593-94. Not all courts or judges are receptive to legislative intent or history arguments. The late Justice Antonin Scalia was probably the most well-known advocate of the "originalists" or "textualists." Textualists believe that looking beyond the text of the given statute and its relation to the larger code, to the supposed "intent" of a multi-membered legislative body, is an inherently flawed method of determining how a statute should be read.

B. Methods of Researching Legislative History

1. State Sources

Legislative history research is best done by working backward from the finished product, a statute. This process is outlined in Table 4-2 and explained below.

Table 4-1. Process of Legislative History Research

Step 1	Identify the session law numbers.
Step 2	Read the session law text.
Step 3	Review the bill chronology and earlier versions of the bill from the Tennessee General Assembly website. For pre-1995 bills, the researcher may create the chronology of events using the *House* and *Senate Journals*.
Step 4	Review any recordings of committee meetings, if available.
Step 5	Review notes from floor debate or actions in House and Senate journals.
Step 6	Read the Governor's signing statement or reported comments if available.

a. Session Law Number

In Tennessee, both of the state codifications of statutory law (*Tennessee Code Annotated* and *West's Tennessee Code Annotated*) and even the free Tennessee Code Unannotated website provide references to the session saws that added and amended the statute you are researching. If you are starting with a citation to a statutory code section, just look up your code citation in any of these codes and note any relevant citations to session laws from those statutory credits.

b. Session Law Text

Identify the session law numbers in the statutory credits at the end of the statute. For example, "Acts 1997, c. 551, § 2" refers to chapter 551, section 2 of the 1997 session laws. Using these references, locate the text of the original session law as passed by the General Assembly and the text of any session laws making subsequent amendments to the statute. The session laws are available in print in many academic law libraries.[11] They are also conveniently online

---

11. Of course, the session laws are only available in print through the 2006 session of the General Assembly, when print publication ceased.

for free at the Secretary of State's website.[12] This online collection of session laws begins for public laws with the 1998–99 Session. The session laws are also variably available on Westlaw, Lexis Advance, and Bloomberg Law as previously discussed. Read the session law text to confirm and identify the part of the session law relevant to the legal issue you are researching.

c. Final Bill and Previous Versions

The text of each session law also includes the bill number for the House or Senate bill that eventually became that session law. Using this bill number, go to the Tennessee General Assembly's archived legislation website[13] and retrieve the bill by linking to the appropriate session, then entering the bill number into the "Bill Number Look-Up" box. The associated bill report is simply a chronological history of the bill as it traveled through the legislative process, not an actual statement about the intent behind the legislation. See Figure 4-1 for an example of a bill report from the General Assembly website. The report may contain links to earlier versions of bills. These various versions of the bill that were rejected or amended through the process may shed light on the legislative intent. While there may not be convenient hypertext links to other related documentation (e.g., committee recordings, the names of the committees and dates of the bill being reported out of committee), the information in the report could be useful in locating these additional documents.

d. Pre-1995 Bills

For pre-1995 bills, a legislative chronology as shown in Table 4-1 must be created by hand using the House and Senate journals. The journals for each session organize bills by public chapter number and include a summary of legislative actions. Academic law libraries and several of the state government libraries have print copies of the Tennessee *House Journals* and *Senate Journals*. At this writing, the journals are difficult to locate on the General Assembly webpage; however, they can be found linked from the Senate and House of Representatives links at the bottom of the main General Assembly webpage. The *Senate Journals* are archived back to the 2003-04 session. However, the *House of Representative Journals* are archived back to 1923. The different versions of the bills, as well as any amendments, must also be located in print.

---

12. The address is http://sos.tn.gov/division-publications/acts-and-resolutions.
13. The address is http://www.capitol.tn.gov/legislation/archives.html.

e. Committee Hearings

Committee hearings have been recorded since the late 1980s. The recordings are available at the Tennessee State Library and Archives; however, they are not transcribed. For more recent years, video recordings may also be available.

f. Floor Debate

The General Assembly provides links for listening to live floor debate in either the Senate or the House. Access is available from the General Assembly homepage. These recordings, however, have been made since 1955 and are available from the Tennessee State Library and Archives.

Although the General Assembly does not provide a verbatim written transcript of floor debate, summaries of floor actions are recorded in the House and Senate journals. Limited online access to the House and Senate journals is available at the General Assembly website, as previously discussed.

g. Governor's Statements

Gubernatorial statements concerning Tennessee legislation are not very common and difficult to locate.[14] The Governor's website[15] provides access to recent written press releases and audio/video releases that might on occasion relate to legislation. The Governor's public statements about legislation might also be recorded by local media, such as *The Tennessean* newspaper.

2. Westlaw, Lexis Advance, and Bloomberg Law as Sources of Legislative History

Westlaw and Lexis Advance provide less precise options for researching Tennessee legislative history. Westlaw provides two databases, "Bill Analysis and other Reports" with various years of coverage, and a "Journals" database of House Journals back to 2000 and Senate Journals back to 2004. To access these databases from the main Westlaw page, select the "State Materials" tab and then the "Tennessee" link. A link to "Tennessee Legislative History" will be available in the right-hand column.

Lexis Advance provides a database, "Tennessee Legislative Bill History," with coverage from 2008 and less comprehensively from 2002; however, there simply may not be much documentation available. The quickest access to this database

---

14. In contrast, presidential signing statements are readily available at the federal level.
15. The address is http://www.tn.gov/governor.

is to enter the database name into the red search box from the main Lexis Advance page.

Bloomberg Law really doesn't provide access to Tennessee legislative history beyond a database of public and private acts.

IV. Federal Legislation

Many volumes have been written about the federal legislative process and how to find federal legislative documents. Due to the limited scope of this chapter, the next few pages will provide only a brief overview of the federal legislative process and how it may be researched. The federal legislative process produces extensive documentation at nearly every stage that is freely available online. Due to this fact, engaging in federal legislative research is usually much easier than engaging in Tennessee legislative research.

A. Summary of the Federal Legislative Process

The federal legislative process, briefly outlined below, mirrors the process in Tennessee.[16]

Federal legislation is created by the introduction of a bill in one (or both) of the chambers of the United States Congress, either the House of Representatives or the Senate. The bill is assigned to a committee where deliberations may occur.

The committee staff may prepare a *committee print* comprised of research, documentation, and other information about the subject of the bill. If hearings are held, transcripts of testimony and statements are created. The committee might submit a report reviewing in detail the elements of the bill, the need for the legislation, and a recommendation for passage. Committee reports are usually the most important statement of legislative intent.

If reported favorably by the committee, the bill moves to the floor of the chamber for debate. Floor debate is transcribed and published in the *Congressional Record*. If the bill is passed by the first chamber, it moves to the second

---

16. For an easy explanation about how our federal statutes are made, see the link to nine short videos from the https://www.congress.gov/ website. For a more detailed and authoritative explanation of how federal legislation is created see "How Our Laws Are Made," revised and updated by John V. Sullivan, Parliamentarian, United States House of Representatives, House Document 110-49, July 2007, also available from the Congress.gov site.

chamber where the process is repeated. This action may happen in sequence, consideration in one chamber and then the other, or it may happen in both chambers simultaneously.

If the second chamber approves the bill in the same form as in the first chamber, the bill is enrolled and sent to the President for signature. If the bill is passed in the second chamber with different amendments, however, then a conference committee must be created to attempt to negotiate the differences. If the conference committee reaches agreement, then the bill is returned to both chambers to be approved and sent to the President for signature.

When presented with a bill passed by Congress, the President may sign the bill into law, ignore the bill (in which case it may become law anyway, depending upon the timing of the legislative session), or veto the bill. If the President signs the bill into law, it becomes a public law and is assigned a public law number such as P.L. 111-148. This was the 148th public law passed in the 111th Congress. Public laws are often given a popular name. The popular name may be included in the public law itself, such as "The Patient Protection and Affordable Care Act" or can arise through use, such as "Obamacare."

The new public law is issued as a *slip law*, which is the first publication of a new act passed by the legislature. At the end of the legislative session, the public laws will be compiled and published in chronological order in *Statutes at Large*. Eventually, the Law Revision Council of the United States House of Representatives will codify the new public law into the *United States Code*.

B. Tracking Current United States Legislation

Researching the current status of federal legislation pending in Congress is a common activity and has benefited greatly from the advent of online access.

1. Using Congress.gov to Track Federal Legislation

Congress.gov is the preeminent website for free federal legislative information that is both currently updated as well as archived. The website provides access to bill reports listing a currently updated, running record of latest activities concerning each bill. Because so much federal legislative history is available digitally, these running records often link directly to the full text of related documentation, such as committee reports, floor debate as published in the *Congressional Record*, amendments, and recorded votes.

Using Congress.gov to find bill reports is relatively simple. The homepage includes a search box for locating bill status by bill number or keywords. The retrieved set of bills leads to summaries for each bill, as well as the sponsor, date of introduction, the latest action taken on the bill, any committee reports, and votes.

Using the bill reports from Congress.gov is the best method of tracking current federal legislation. See Figure 4-2 for an example of a bill report created at the Congress.gov website concerning H.R. 1321 from the 114th Congress, to amend the Federal Food, Drug, and Cosmetic Act to ban cosmetics that contain synthetic plastic microbeads beginning January 1, 2018.

Figure 4-2. A Congress.gov-Created Report Concerning H.R. 1321 — from 114th Congress (2015–16)

Title: Microbead-Free Waters Act of 2015

Sponsor: Rep. Pallone, Frank, Jr. [D-NJ-6] (Introduced 03/04/2015)

Committees: House—Energy and Commerce

Committee Reports: H. Rept. 114-371

Latest Action: 12/28/2015 Became Public Law No: 114-114. (All Actions)

Actions Overview: H.R.1321 — 114th Congress (2015–2016)

Bill History — Congressional Record References

Actions Overview [7]

All Actions Except Amendments [20]

All Actions

7 results for Actions Overview

Date	Actions Overview
12/28/2015	**Became Public Law No: 114-114.**
12/28/2015	Signed by President.
12/22/2015	Presented to President.
12/18/2015	Passed/agreed to in Senate: Passed Senate without amendment by Unanimous Consent.
12/07/2015	Passed/agreed to in House: On motion to suspend the rules and pass the bill, as amended Agreed to by voice vote. (text: CR H9021)
12/07/2015	Reported (Amended) by the Committee on Energy and Commerce. H. Rept. 114-371.
03/04/2015	Introduced in House.

Source: Congress.gov, https://www.congress.gov/bill/114th-congress/house-bill/1321.

2. Other Online Sources for Tracking Federal Legislation

Although Congress.gov is the best source for federal bill tracking, there are several other options.

a. Govtrack.us

Govtrack.us provides timely notification via email or RSS of congressional actions on a bill. It will also track actions of a member of Congress or the activity of a particular committee. You can track documents that have particular combinations of words, relate to an individual bill number, or affect a U.S. Code section.

b. Westlaw

Use the "Federal Bill Tracking" database for summaries and the current status of pending legislation in the United States Congress. Like Congress.gov, this database is updated daily. Westlaw also provides historical bill tracking, a running record for bills introduced in previous legislative sessions beginning in 1991.

c. Lexis Advance

Lexis Advance includes bill tracking information in the "Congressional Bill Tracking" database. Historical running records of bills are found for previous sessions of Congress back to 1989.

d. Bloomberg Law

Bloomberg Law provides databases of current bills and historical bills back to 1993. To access these databases, and related databases of federal legislative history material, choose "Federal Law" from the "Research" pane on the main Bloomberg Law page, then "Federal Legislative," then "U.S. Congress." For currently pending bills, choose the "Track Bill" option to be notified by email of any legislative changes involving the bill.

C. Researching Federal Legislative History

1. Why Research Federal Legislative History?

Interpreting statutes is perhaps even more challenging at the federal level where there are often more diverse and competing interests in the legislative process that may affect the final language of legislation. While judges differ in the importance they grant legislative history in interpreting statutes, many courts have relied upon clues to legislative intent that have arisen from the legislative process.

Federal legislative history is also challenging because there are many more documents to consult. Fortunately, there are also more sophisticated research tools available. Remember that a single code section can be the end result of many session laws. To do thorough legislative history research, you must determine which session laws enacted or changed the particular part of code at issue.

2. Legislative History Available in the Annotated Codes

West's United States Code Annotated, whether on Westlaw or in print, provides references and sometimes links to the full text of relevant legislative history documents. While examining a particular USCA code section through Westlaw, select the "History" tab. The "Editor's and Revisor's Notes" section of the tab provides a short summary of the changes made by each session law, allowing you to select the relevant session law. The "Legislative History" section of the tab provides a list of documents available on Westlaw for each session law that affected the code section. In contrast, the *United States Code Service*, both in print or through Lexis Advance, currently lacks the depth of detail and links to extensive, relevant legislative history compared to Westlaw. It does provide the "History" section at the end of each section, listing all the session laws involved in creating the code section, and some brief notes explaining the changes made by each session law.

3. Compiled Histories

The most important shortcut to researching federal legislative histories is to use a professionally prepared, compiled legislative history. A number of publishers compile and publish complete legislative histories that include all legislative documentation related to a public law. Law libraries collect these publications, and they are usually well indexed. Although there are no free online collections of compiled legislative histories, Westlaw, Lexis Advance, and HeinOnline are increasingly adding compiled legislative histories for major public laws to their online collections in individual databases. For example, Westlaw provides an extensive collection of compiled legislative histories on a variety of topics in the "U.S. GAO Federal Legislative Histories" database.

4. Committee Reports

If a compiled legislative history is not available, the next best option is to find the committee report. Committee reports, widely viewed as the most important piece of legislative history, are readily available on Congress.gov back to 1995. Selected reports are available back to the 1940s on Westlaw and 1990 on Lexis Advance.

5. Collecting Your Own Legislative History

Just as in Tennessee, collecting the legislative history of a federal public law is a time consuming task. It is made easier, however, by the superior documentation of the process and the online accessibility of the various types of documentation.

Similar to the process in Tennessee, it is usually easiest to work backwards to collect legislative history documents. The best starting point at the federal level is a statute, preferably from an annotated code. Immediately after the text of the statute in the code, you will find legislative history notes that will include both the *Statutes at Large* and public law citations for the legislation that affected the statute to be researched; these citations will assist in identifying the session law relevant to the code text that interests you. Alternatively, you may find the same information by using the "Popular Name Table" in any of the United States Code versions, where the popular names of public laws are arranged alphabetically. Beside each popular name is the USC citation, and citations to the public law number and *Statutes at Large* citations for legislation affecting the statute being researched.

Working either online or in print, you may use these citations to find specific, related documents. For example, Congress.gov would be a good source to use for recent committee reports or pages from the *Congressional Record* concerning floor debate. See Figure 4-2 for an example of a report from Congress.gov and how it links to additional documentation.

For a summarized comparison of the Tennessee and federal research process and sources, see Table 4-2.

Table 4-2. Comparison of Sources for Tennessee and Federal Legislative History

ACTION	TENNESSEE SOURCES	FEDERAL SOURCES
Introduction of Bills	**Bills** are introduced by legislators. *Published at the General Assembly website (http://www.capitol.tn.gov).*	**Bills** are introduced by legislators. *Published at the Congress.gov website.*
Committee Work	**Audio recordings** of some committees from the late 1980s. *Available at the Tennessee State Library and Archives.* All committees and subcommittees have been recorded since 2006. *Video recordings may also be available for recent years, and are typically linked from the web-based legislative history on the General Assembly website.*	**Committee prints** (documentation of related information by committee staffers). **Committee hearings** (transcripts of witness testimony and other statements). **Committee reports** (the most persuasive piece of legislative history). *Generally available from Congress.gov*
Floor Debate	**Audio recording** of General Assembly floor debates began in 1955. These are available at the Tennessee State Library and Archives. Current floor debate in the General Assembly is also available as a streaming video broadcast from the General Assembly website with limited archiving of recordings. **House Journals** and **Senate Journals** may contain some mention of topics of discussion. *Generally available at the General Assembly website.*	**Congressional Record** publishes the recorded debates on the floor of the U.S. House and Senate each day. *Available from Congress.gov back to 1995.*
Session Laws	**Tennessee Acts** *Available* from 1997 at the Secretary of State's website http://sos.tn.gov/division-publications/acts-and-resolutions	**Statutes at Large**
Codified Law	**Tennessee Code Annotated** **West's Tennessee Code Annotated** *Available on Westlaw.* **Tennessee Code Unannotated** *Available at* http://www.lexisnexis.com/hottopics/tncode/	**United States Code** (official) **United States Code Annotated** *Available on Westlaw.* **United States Code Service** *Available on Lexis Advance.*

Chapter 5

Researching Administrative Law

Administrative agencies are part of the executive branch of government, but they are granted powers that mimic the powers of all three branches of government.[1] Agencies have quasi-legislative power, including drafting rules to interpret and implement legislative and executive mandates; quasi-executive power, including issuing licenses, investigating whether rules are being followed, and enforcing rules; and quasi-judicial power, including decision-making when a party objects to the rules or implementation of the rules.

Agencies create administrative law, which is composed of rules and decisions.[2] What appears to be a broad expanse of agency authority, however, is actually narrowly tailored to accomplish specific tasks. Every administrative rule, for example, must be authorized by other primary law, usually statutory law. An administrative rule is invalid if it exceeds the authority granting the agency the power to create the rule. Administrative authority usually comes from the legislature in the form of *enabling acts*.

Administrative law directly affects many aspects of daily life. Examples of Tennessee administrative rules include rules setting standards for handling radioactive materials as well as rules specifying the required contents of a kit each cosmetology student must have after 200 hours of enrollment in a cosmetology school in Tennessee.[3] Examples of federal administrative rules range from procedures for homeland security to rules requiring that iodized salt con-

---

1. Much of this chapter draws on *North Carolina Legal Research*, which is used with permission. Parts V and VI of this chapter copy the discussion of federal administrative law from that book, again with permission.

2. Generally, administrative regulations are referred to as "rules" at the state level and "regulations" at the federal level. However, you might also see the two terms used interchangeably. They refer to the same type of law.

3. Tenn. Comp. R. & Regs. 0400-20-04-.01 et seq. and 0440-01-.07(1), respectively.

tainers include the statement "this salt supplies iodide, a necessary nutrient" on each package in specified size font.[4]

This chapter begins with research into Tennessee administrative law; then the chapter turns research into federal administrative law.

I. Tennessee Administrative Law

Administrative law initially developed without a uniform process, and was not well structured or widely distributed. With few exceptions, agencies drafted their own regulations and made them available at agency offices. The general public lacked both input in the rulemaking process and convenient access to the rules. In the mid-1940s the federal government created the first federal "Administrative Procedures Act" addressing this issue at the federal level. Although slower at the state level, most states followed a similar pattern eventually adopting a version of the model state administrative procedures act. Tennessee's Uniform Administrative Procedures Act was first enacted in the 1970s and has been substantially amended several times.[5] The act defines the process through which administrative rules are created, the procedures to be followed in administrative hearings, and how the information is organized and published.

A. Rules

In Tennessee, the term "rule" includes "each agency statement of general applicability that implements or prescribes law or policy or describes the procedures or practice requirements of any agency and also includes the amendment or repeal of a prior rule."[6] Rules created within the scope of authority following the process prescribed by the Uniform Administrative Procedures Act have the full force and effect of law.[7]

1. General Process of Creating Administrative Rules

In Tennessee, the term "agency" may include the following types of organizations: a department, a commission, a state board, "or any other unit of state

---

4. 21 C.F.R. § 100.155 (2015).
5. Tenn. Code Ann. § 4-5-101 et seq.
6. Tenn. Code Ann. § 4-5-102 (12) (2015).
7. *Kogan v. Tenn. Bd. of Dentistry*, No. M2003-00291-COA-R3-CV, 2003 WL 23093863, at *5 (Tenn. Ct. App. Dec. 30, 2003) (citing *Houck v. Minton*, 212 S.W.2d 891, 895 (Tenn. 1948)).

government authorized or required by any statute or constitutional provision to make rules or to determine contested cases."[8]

Agencies are responsible for creating and maintaining appropriate administrative rules to facilitate their work. These activities may include proposing new rules or making amendments to existing rules under their control. Additionally, any municipality, corporation, or any five or more persons having an interest in a rule may petition an agency to adopt a new rule or change an existing rule.[9]

Generally, a Tennessee agency has several procedural options when creating a new rule or amending an existing rule. The process begins with the agency drafting a proposed rule and sending notice of the intent to create a new rule to the Tennessee Secretary of State. An agency may choose (unless statutorily required) whether to have a public hearing to discuss the proposed rule.

If an agency plans a public hearing, then along with the notice, the agency must include the time and place of the hearing, the express terms of the rule being proposed, and statutory authority for the rule.[10] A rule being created by this method is referred to as a "rulemaking hearing rule." The Secretary of State, having received this notice, must publish this information to the Administrative Register website[11] within seven days of receiving it. Notice through this method of publication must be given at least forty-five days prior to the hearing. The method of conducting the hearings is prescribed by statute.[12] The agency must fully consider all information submitted concerning the proposed rules and, if requested, must issue a concise statement of the reasons for its action.[13]

If not otherwise required to have a public hearing, an administrative agency may choose to avoid a public hearing by including (along with the express terms of the rule being proposed and statutory authority) a statement in the notice that the agency will adopt the proposed rule without a public hearing after ninety days, unless within that time the agency receives:

1) A petition for a public hearing filed by at least ten persons who will be affected by the rule; or

2) A petition filed by an association of ten or more members; or

---

8. Tenn. Code Ann. § 4-5-102 (2) (2015).

9. Tenn. Code Ann. § 4-5-201 (2015).

10. Tenn. Code Ann. § 4-5-203 (2015).

11. The Administrative Register's website is http://www.tennessee.gov/sos/pub/tar/index.htm.

12. Tenn. Code Ann. § 4-5-204 (2015).

13. Tenn. Code Ann. § 4-5-205 (2015).

3) A petition filed by a municipality; or

4) Notice of a majority vote of any standing committee of the General Assembly in favor of a public hearing.

If an agency receives such notice requesting a public hearing, the agency must forward the request to the Secretary of State and a public hearing must be held as described in the paragraph above.[14] A rule being created using this method is simply referred to as a "proposed rule."

A third option for rulemaking is available to an agency if the proposed rule qualifies as an emergency rule. An emergency rule complying with the statutory requirements may become effective immediately but may only be effective for up to 180 days.[15]

Before a final rule can be filed with the Secretary of State to be codified, the rule must be submitted to the Tennessee Attorney General for a review of the legality and constitutionality of the rule and either approved or disapproved.[16]

Once a final rule (or change to an existing rule) is approved by the Attorney General, the last step in the process is for the rule is filed with the Secretary of State for codification in the "Official Compilation of the Rules and Regulations of the State of Tennessee."

2. *Tennessee Administrative Code*

Two publications mentioned in the rulemaking process above provide important information about Tennessee administrative rules. The first publication, the "Official Compilation Rules and Regulations of the State of Tennessee," is Tennessee's administrative code, where rules from 119 agencies, boards, and other administrative bodies are codified (organized by subject and currently updated) by the Secretary of State. While the "Official Compilation of the Rules and Regulations of the State of Tennessee" is the official title of the administrative code, they are also referred to as the "Effective Rules and Regulations of the State of Tennessee."

The codified administrative rules in Tennessee are designated by a number in the form 0000-00-00.00. The first four digits are the agency chapter number. The administrative rule in Figure 5-1 starts with 0240, which refers to the Tennessee Board of Regents. The second and third sets of numbers work to group a related series of regulations together in chapters.

---

14. Tenn. Code Ann. § 4-5-202(2) (2015)
15. Tenn. Code Ann. § 4-5-208 (2015)
16. Tenn. Code Ann. § 4-5-211 (2015)

Figure 5-1. Example of Tennessee Administrative Regulation Numbering

0240-01:	Statewide Administrative Rules
0240-02:	System-Wide Student Rules
0240-02-02:	Out-of-State Students
0240-02-02-.04:	Out-of-State Students Who Are Not Required to Pay Out-of-State Tuition
0240-02-02-.07:	Procedure for Appealing Classification
0240-03:	Institutional Student Disciplinary Rules
0240-04:	Institutional Student Housing Rules

Source: Official Compilation of the Rules and Regulations of the State of Tennessee 0240-01 to 0240-04.

Within 0240-02, regulations at 0240-02-2 deal with classifying students as in-state or out-of-state. Regulation 0240-02-2-.04 describes out-of-state students who are not required to pay out-of-state tuition, and Regulation 0240-02-2-.07 deals with the procedure for students to appeal their classification as in-state or out-of-state. The specific regulations within chapter 0249-02-02 are shown in Figure 5-2.

Figure 5-2. Sample Tennessee Regulatory Chapter

RULES OF THE TENNESSEE BOARD OF REGENTS
STATE UNIVERSITY AND COMMUNITY COLLEGE SYSTEM OF
TENNESSEE SYSTEMWIDE STUDENT RULES
CHAPTER 0240-02-02
CLASSIFYING STUDENTS IN-STATE AND OUT-OF-STATE
TABLE OF CONTENTS

0240-02-02-.01	Intent
0240-02-02-.02	Definitions
0240-02-02-.03	Rules for Determination of Status
0240-02-02-.04	Out-of-State Students Who Are Not Required to Pay Out-Of-State Tuition
0240-02-02-.05	Presumption
0240-02-02-.06	Evidence to be Considered for Establishment of Domicile
0240-02-02-.07	Appeal
0240-02-02-.08	Effective Date for Reclassification
0240-02-02-.09	Effective Date

Source: Official Compilation of the Rules and Regulations of the State of Tennessee 0240-02-02.

The free, online version of the administrative code available at the Secretary of State's website[17] is the official compilation of Tennessee administrative regulations[18] While the rules found at this website are official, currently updated, and browsable, they are challenging to search using keywords.

Tennessee's administrative code is also browsable and more effectively keyword searchable at Westlaw, Lexis Advance, and Bloomberg Law. Westlaw offers historical databases of previous codes since 2002, and Lexis Advance has archived administrative codes from Tennessee starting in 2004. Bloomberg Law does not offer historical versions of Tennessee regulations.

3. Tennessee Administrative Register

The second publication important for state administrative law research is the Tennessee Administrative Register, which is also freely and officially available from the Tennessee Secretary of State's website.[19] As described in the section above about creating administrative rules, the Register's general role is to serve as public notice of administrative rulemaking. The Register contains Rulemaking Hearing Notices, the text of pending rules, emergency rules, and other relevant announcements. The website includes archives of rule filings and rulemaking hearing notices back to 2005. The Register is updated with new information within five days of filing with the Secretary of State's Office.

Information from the Tennessee Administrative Register is variously available from Westlaw, Lexis Advance, and Bloomberg Law, through regulation tracking databases with coverage for the last several years. Westlaw also includes a database of proposed regulations with selected coverage back to 2006.

B. Administrative Decisions

In addition to the quasi-legislative authority to promulgate rules, agencies also have quasi-judicial authority to settle disputes between aggrieved individuals and the agency, known as *contested cases*.[20] Agencies generally have one or two informal opportunities to settle disputes. A citizen who disagrees with the outcome may then file a contested case with the Administrative Hearings Division

---

17. The address is http://sos.tn.gov/effective-rules.

18. Tenn. Code Ann. § 4-5-221 (2015). The print version of the administrative code ceased publication in 2004 and the code is now only found online.

19. The address is http://sos.tn.gov/products/division-publications/administrative-register.

20. Tenn. Code Ann. § 4-5-102(3) (2015).

of the Tennessee Department of State. An administrative law judge (ALJ), not employed by the regulating agency, will be appointed to hear the case. The rules governing the proceedings of a contested case can be found at Tenn. Code Ann. § 4-5-301 et seq. The ALJ will issue a hearing decision to both the citizen and the agency. The agency will make the final agency decision. If a citizen chooses, she may appeal the agency decision to chancery court.[21]

II. Researching Tennessee Administrative Rules

Finding relevant Tennessee administrative rules is notoriously difficult for two reasons. First, codifications of administrative rules are typically not well indexed, if at all. Second, the complex, detailed, and precise nature of the terminology involved makes identifying search terms difficult, whether browsing or selecting search terms to use in a full-text, keyword search.

A. Starting with a Citation to a Rule from a Secondary Authority

A secondary authority can be an effective tool for finding references to administrative rules. For example, a law review article or a Tennessee treatise addressing a relevant topic of Tennessee law might provide a citation to the relevant administrative rules. Even if the secondary authority does not refer directly to the relevant rules, the discussion might provide citations to relevant statutory law. This discussion might lead to administrative rule citations in the statutory annotations. Finally, even if the secondary authorities do not provide citations to rules or related statutes, the discussion in the secondary authority itself should provide clues about relevant search terms to use in a more direct and effective keyword search of the rules, if that becomes necessary.

B. Starting with a Citation from an Authorizing or Enabling Statute

The annotated statutory codes in Tennessee are also effective starting points for administrative law research. The *Tennessee Code Annotated* is published by LexisNexis and available on Lexis Advance, and *West's Tennessee Code Annotated* is published by West and available on Westlaw. Regulations must be authorized

---

21. Tenn. Code Ann. § 4-5-322 (2015).

by statutory law, so an annotated version of the enabling act providing that authority would likely cite the related administrative rules.

C. Browsing Titles in Print or Online

Another approach to finding administrative rules is browsing the administrative code titles. This approach is most effective when you are more familiar with the research issue and preferably when you have used the administrative code to research this issue recently. One danger in this approach is missing relevant material that is hidden in another title whose name might not suggest its relevance to the subject being researched.

D. Searching the Administrative Code Online in Full Text or by Field or Segment

A final approach is to search the full text of the administrative code on Westlaw, Lexis Advance, or Bloomberg. You might narrow this search by selecting fields or segments of the code, and using keywords. Again, the important concern here is that you know the precise language that will be used in the text you want to retrieve. Otherwise, the text will not be retrieved since the search software is only searching for word matches, not concept matches.

E. Using the *Tennessee Register* to Update

To determine the most current status of an administrative rule, after identifying the rule in the administrative code, simply browse the Administrative Register website to determine whether there are any "pending rules" or "rule-making hearing notices" being considered, or perhaps already adopted but not yet codified in the administrative code, that could affect the rules and issues you are researching.

III. Researching Tennessee Administrative Decisions

Orders issued by administrative judges as a result of contested case hearings are currently being archived through the efforts of the University of Tennessee College of Law Library and the University's online repository, TRACE. You may search or browse the decisions directly from the TRACE website[22] or access

---

22. The address is http://trace.tennessee.edu/utk_lawopinions.

them from a link at the Secretary of State's Administrative Hearings website.[23] This collection extends from 2005 and is updated at least monthly.

Extremely limited coverage of Tennessee administrative law decisions is available from Westlaw, Lexis Advance, and Bloomberg Law, with very few agencies' decisions included.

IV. Tennessee Attorney General Opinions

The Tennessee Attorney General is required by statute to issue opinions on questions of law submitted by members of the General Assembly, the Governor, Secretary of State, Comptroller of the Treasury, or other state officers in the conduct of their business.[24] While opinions of the Attorney General are not law, they represent the state's interpretation of the law applied to a specific question. They are very persuasive and courts defer to them.[25]

The most convenient and least expensive method of researching Attorney General opinions is to use the Tennessee Office of the Attorney General's website to browse or keyword search the opinions.[26] The collection contains opinions issued beginning in 2000. Researchers may also contact the office directly for copies of opinions that are not available online.

Other sources of Tennessee Attorney General opinions include Westlaw and Lexis Advance, both with coverage back to 1977, but they are not available on Bloomberg Law.

V. Federal Administrative Law

Federal administrative law is created and operates in much the same manner as Tennessee administrative law. The first federal code of administrative law was published in 1938. The first federal Administrative Procedures Act was enacted in 1946 for the purpose of requiring agencies to keep the public informed of agency organization, procedures, and regulations. The act also provided a

---

23. The address is http://sos.tn.gov/apd.

24. Tenn. Code Ann. §8-6-109(b)(6) (2015).

25. *Scott v. Ashland Healthcare Ctr., Inc.*, 49 S.W.3d 281, 287 (Tenn. 2001), quoting *State v. Black*, 897 S.W.2d 680, 683 (Tenn. 1995) ("Although opinions of the Attorney General are not binding on courts, government officials rely upon them for guidance; therefore, this opinion is entitled to considerable deference.").

26. The address is http://attorneygeneral.tn.gov/op/opinions.html.

method for public participation in the rulemaking process, standardized the rulemaking process, and confirmed the idea of judicial review of administrative decisions.

Unlike Tennessee administrative rules, at the federal level the administrative rules are referred to as administrative "regulations." Federal administrative regulations have the full force and effect of law when created within the parameters of the Administrative Procedures Act.[27]

A. Federal Administrative Regulations

Federal regulations are created in a similar manner as Tennessee rules. Upon receiving authority to draft rules governing a specific issue, an agency will investigate and use its expertise to propose regulations. The proposed regulations are published in the *Federal Register*. The public has a specific period of time in which to respond. The agency may hold one or more public hearings about the proposed regulations. Regulations.gov is a website where the public may conveniently find, view, and comment on proposed federal regulations. The agency will consider the public feedback and then issue final regulations, which also must be published in the *Federal Register*. Thereafter, the final regulations will be codified in the *Code of Federal Regulations*.

1. *Code of Federal Regulations*

The *Code of Federal Regulations* (CFR) is a compilation of all the federal administrative regulations currently in effect. It is arranged by agency, which is a rough arrangement by subject. The CFR is comprised of fifty titles, in a similar manner as the United States Code's fifty-four titles. While some of the titles between the CFR and USC correspond, like Title 26 addressing the Internal Revenue Service, more often than not the correlation does not exist. As discussed later, however, that does not keep the United States Code from being a good source for finding relevant regulations. Each title of the CFR is organized by chapter, part, and section. Chapters are often not used in identifying specific regulations. For the following example, 20 CFR § 416.906, 20 is the title, 416 is the part, and the section is .906. Often, when speaking of the section, the part is excluded. A lawyer might say "Title 20 CFR section 416.906."

The CFR is published annually in paperback form by the Government Publishing Office. Rather than publishing the entire set at one time, GPO publishes

---

27. *Atchison, T. & S.F. Ry. Co. v. Scarlett*, 300 U.S. 471 (1937).

one quarter of it every three months so that the entire set is republished over the course of a year. Titles 1-16 are updated and republished January 1 of each year; Titles 17-27 are updated on April 1; Titles 28-41 are updated as of July 1; and Titles 42-50 are updated every October 1. The paper covers of the individual volumes change color each year, which makes identifying the volumes that have been updated much easier. Often, the volumes are months late being updated and distributed, and many volumes straggle from the publisher at different times, even volumes addressing parts of the same title. In addition to printing the CFR, the Government Publishing Office also posts the CFR on its Federal Digital System (FDsys) website.[28]

You should note that GPO is in the process of developing a new website, govinfo.gov,[29] that will eventually replace the seven-year-old Federal Digital System. Currently, govinfo.gov is in beta. Upon its release, govinfo.gov will be a new front door to all of the same information that was available at FDsys.[30] Govinfo.gov will likely be released from beta sometime in 2017, although no date has yet been given.

The new website, redesigned and mobile-friendly, includes several new features and incorporates state-of-the-art technologies. Notable new features include a modern look and feel, an open-source search engine with enhancements to the search filters, the capability to link related content, and more options for sharing pages and content on social media.

Currently, everything that is available at FDsys is also available by searching at govinfo.gov. Everything may not yet be browsable at govinfo.gov as of this writing. Eventually, browsability at govinfo.gov will be improved from FDsys with two new ways to browse content, alphabetically and by category. For purposes of this book, however, rest assured that whenever something is identified as being available at FDsys, it is also available at govinfo.gov.

At this writing, the text of the CFR at the FDsys website is generally no more current than the print copy. GPO also produces the Electronic Code of Federal Regulations (e-CFR), which is a more current, convenient and authentic but *unofficial* editorial compilation of the CFR incorporating the latest amendments as published in the *Federal Register*.[31] e-CFR is a project of GPO and the National Archives and Records Administration's Office of the Federal Reg-

---

28. The Federal Digital System is available at http://www.gpo.gov/fdsys.
29. The address is https://govinfo.gov.
30. The address is https://govinfo.gov/features/news/meet-govinfo.
31. The address is http://www.ecfr.gov.

ister. It is typically updated and current within several days of any changes published in the *Federal Register* affecting currently codified regulations.

Westlaw, Lexis Advance, and Bloomberg Law also each provide a fee-based CFR database that, like GPO's e-CFR, is updated within days of changes published in the *Federal Register*. All three services also provide some case law annotations. Additionally, Westlaw provides an annotated CFR database that includes a "Context & Analysis" tab for each section of the CFR. This tab compiles citations to any relevant law review articles, *United States Code Annotated* sections, or *Federal Register* summaries.

2. *Federal Register*

The *Federal Register* serves the same purpose as the *Tennessee Register*. It is published and printed every business day, however, rather than simply posted and updated on the government website. The *Federal Register* serves as the official publication of proposed and final regulations, as well as notices from federal agencies and some Presidential documents such as executive orders. It is available in print as well as online.[32] In addition to the densely packed, traditional, small print *Federal Register*, there is also a user-friendly web version.[33] This 2.0 version is much more interactive and colorful than the official version. However, for any legal research project where accuracy is important, it is best to use the government's official version of the *Federal Register* which is available in PDF form and archived back to 1994. This official version is updated every day by 6:00 a.m. It is freely available and both browsable and searchable. Westlaw, Lexis Advance, and Bloomberg Law also provide online access through currently updated databases that are fee-based.

3. Researching Federal Administrative Regulations

Researching a legal subject in the print version of the CFR is challenging. As with Tennessee rules, researching federal regulations is best begun in secondary authorities. Reading more about a legal issue in secondary authorities might actually produce citations to relevant regulations. Alternatively, citations to relevant United States Code sections might be revealed in secondary authorities that would be helpful in the research process. Lastly, the understanding and terminology gained from the secondary authority will only improve

---

32. The address is https://www.gpo.gov/fdsys/browse/collection.action?collection-Code=FR.

33. The address is https://www.federalregister.gov.

your ability to conduct effective full-text, keyword searches in the CFR, if necessary.

Because the United States Code is generally easier to search than the CFR, the next best starting point for legal subject searching would be the *United States Code Service* or the *United States Code Annotated*. These annotated codes should provide citations to relevant regulations. Historically, the *United States Code Service* has done a superior job connecting the statutes to the regulations.

Additional options for searching for relevant regulations include browsing the CFR titles and chapters, or using the single-volume index found in the last volume of the CFR set. The title names are not always helpful in identifying the scope of regulations they contain. The index only indexes regulations down to the more general "part" level rather than the narrower "section" level and is notoriously not very detailed. When using the index, you must locate the part and then browse the list of sections in the specific volume to find the most relevant sections.

Online options for researching federal regulations abound. The freely available, online version of the CFR from GPO's Federal Digital System (or the new govinfo.gov website currently under development) is browsable and searchable by keyword, citation, or title. Use of this database is highly recommended. GPO's e-CFR is also useful, especially due to its current updating, although it's not the official version.

The Westlaw, Lexis Advance, and Bloomberg Law versions of the CFR are also currently updated and provide keyword-search and title-browsable access. Westlaw also provides one superior alternative method of searching, a browsable CFR index, providing an excellent approach to the CFR.

B. Updating Federal Administrative Regulations

1. Online

The best way to update a federal regulation is to use e-CFR, from the Federal Digital System (FDsys), as the starting point. This resource should provide the date through which the most recent changes to regulations were last incorporated into the text. Next, locate the *Federal Register* issues at FDsys that have been published since the most recent incorporation date from e-CFR. Examine the "CFR Sections Affected" chart in the most recent issue of the *Federal Register* to make sure your section has not been amended. A similar method should be used if updating the CFR database from Westlaw, Lexis Advance, or Bloomberg Law, based upon the last date the CFR database was updated.

2. Print

Updating the print version of the CFR is more challenging. This updating challenge extends to the digital annual (non e-CFR) CFR database at the government's FDsys website that is no more current than the print version. Regardless of the source, assuming the title is more than one month past publication, there is a two-step process for updating a paper regulation. The updating process is similar to checking pocket parts, except that you will use a separate publication called the *List of Sections Affected* (LSA) and the back page of the *Federal Register*.

a. List of Sections Affected *Monthly Pamphlet*

First, find the most recent pamphlet (or database on FDsys) known as the *List of Sections Affected* (LSA). LSA is a monthly publication that lists all sections of the CFR that have been affected by recent rulemaking activity. Information in the LSA should be current back to the publication date of your paper CFR volume; however, you should cautiously confirm the dates of coverage for the LSA publication or database to ensure coverage.

If there is no reference to a section containing your regulation in the LSA, there have been no changes to your regulation between the date the CFR title was last published and the date of the LSA. If, however, there has been a change, this table will list the *Federal Register* page number for each new agency action that has affected your specific section.

b. Federal Register *"CFR Parts Affected" Table*

The second step involves examining a table in the back of the *Federal Register*. The table is called the "CFR Parts Affected for [the current month]." Search the table for reference to your CFR section. Search this table in each *Federal Register* issue published on the last day of each month since the most recently published, monthly LSA.

When you reach the current month, search this same table in the most recent *Federal Register* issue. The chart in the back of the *Federal Register* is always cumulative for the entire month. If you use the free online issues of *Federal Register* at the FDsys website, which are updated each morning by 6:00 a.m., this process will update your regulation to same-day currency. The paper *Federal Register* will probably be a week or two old due to mailing and processing.

In addition to this method of updating, you should also use citators such as Shepard's on Lexis Advance or KeyCite on Westlaw to find all related information citing a specific regulation being researched.

C. Administrative Decisions

As with Tennessee agencies, federal agencies issue a number of types and levels of decisions. Federal administrative decisions are much more variable and widely dispersed. Agency decisions were traditionally published in individual agency print reporters. For example, *Federal Trade Commission Decisions* is a reporter for the decisions of the Federal Trade Commission. A number of agency decisions were also published in private publications by publishers such as Commerce Clearing House (CCH) and Bureau of National Affairs (BNA).

Most recent federal agency decisions are being published directly at the agency websites. For example, the Federal Trade Commission now provides access to commission decisions back to 1969. Agency websites are independent and also vary widely in terms of organization and information provided. These websites can easily be found online using a search engine such as Google. Alternatively, you may use a collection of links to "Administrative Decisions" posted by the University of Virginia Library.[34] This site might be particularly useful if you do not initially know which agency might publish the decisions you need or you are uncertain of the level of decision you need from a large agency. Recent agency decisions are also selectively available in fee-based databases Westlaw, Lexis Advance, and Bloomberg Law.

Once all administrative remedies have been exhausted, dissatisfied parties may have the opportunity to appeal an administrative decision to federal court. Once the issues from a specific administrative decision enter the federal court system, researching the issues becomes case law research, which is addressed in Chapter 2.

VI. Researching U.S. Attorney General Opinions

The Office of the United States Attorney General was created by the Judiciary Act of 1789. The Attorney General is the head of the Justice Department (created in 1870) and serves as the chief law enforcement officer of the federal government. Among other duties, the U.S. Attorney General gives advice and issues opinions upon request to the President and the heads of the executive departments of the federal government. The Attorney General has delegated to the U.S. Department of Justice Office of Legal Counsel the duty of providing

---

34. The address is http://guides.lib.virginia.edu/administrative_decisions.

legal advice to the President and executive branch agencies. This includes drafting the formal opinions of the Attorney General.[35]

The opinions (some back to 1934) may be found for free at the Office of Legal Counsel website.[36] They are browsable by year. They are also available on Westlaw, Lexis Advance, and Bloomberg Law, which all provide access back to 1791. Just as with opinions of the Tennessee Attorney General, opinions of the U.S. Attorney General are only persuasive as an educated interpretation of law applied to specific facts. The opinions are not the law itself.

35. For a discussion of how Attorney General Opinions are researched, drafted, and published, See "Memorandum for Attorneys of the Office, RE: Best Practices for OLC Legal Advice and Written Opinions," http://www.justice.gov/olc/best-practices-olc-legal-advice-and-written-opinions.

36. The address is http://www.justice.gov/olc/opinions.

Chapter 6

Updating Research

I. Introduction to Updating

Before using any legal authority to analyze a problem, you must know how that authority has been treated by later actions of a court, legislature, or agency. A case may have been reversed or overruled; a statute may have been amended or repealed. Ensuring that the cases, statutes, and other authorities you rely on represent the *current* law requires updating your research using a citator service. This updating process is still sometimes referred to as "Shepardizing" because the first major updating tool was *Shepard's Citations*.

Checking to see whether your authorities are still good law is crucial, but it is not the only reason to use a citator service. You should also use citator services to expand your research by finding references to additional authorities addressing the same legal issues and to assist your own understanding of the prior and subsequent histories of the authorities you will rely on.

Citator services compile lists of citations to legal sources that have cited a particular authority. If you want to update a case opinion, for example, you could enter the citation in the *Shepard's* service on LexisNexis, the *KeyCite* service on Westlaw, or the *BCite* service on Bloomberg Law. Any of those citator services will then provide you with a list of authorities that cited your case, together with codes or symbols that tell you how your case was treated by those authorities. The online services also provide easy access to information about the prior and subsequent history of the case.[1]

After a discussion of the ethics of updating and an overview of fundamental concepts, this chapter explains how to update a case with Shepard's, KeyCite,

---

1. The original *Shepard's Citations* was a set of print books where you looked up your citation and then read through columns of hieroglyphics deciphering its later treatment. Shepard's books are still printed, but are always significantly behind the online updating services, and are therefore not recommended as a way to ensure the currency of authorities.

and BCite, as well as less robust tools on Fastcase and Google Scholar. The chapter concludes with brief discussions of updating statutes and other authorities.

II. Ethics in Updating[2]

Updating is a time-consuming activity, primarily because of the large number of sources you must read and analyze. But competent research requires updating, and your research is not finished until this step has been completed for each authority that you use in your legal analysis. Courts expect lawyers to update their research to ensure that their arguments are supported and to present the current state of the law in their filings. One federal court has noted that it is "really inexcusable" for any lawyer to fail to routinely use a citator service to update his or her work.[3] Failing to cite current law or disclose adverse authority may result in sanctions, malpractice suits, public embarrassment, and damage to your reputation, both within your firm and office and in the larger legal community. In one instance, a judge ordered a major law firm provide each of its lawyers a copy of an opinion chastising the firm for failing to cite a case adverse to the client's argument.[4] In another case, an attorney was found to have willfully abused the judicial process and was ordered to pay over $14,000 in fees to the opposing party when he filed a complaint in reliance upon a case that was no longer good law. The court commented, when explaining its decision to impose the award of fees, that the attorney "never Shepardized his principle authority," and concluded with references to the attorney's "laziness, greed, [or] incompetence."[5]

III. Nuts and Bolts of Updating[6]

Shepard's, KeyCite, and BCite share some common features. First, important terminology is similar. The authority being updated, for example, a case opinion, is called the *document*. The citator will list for you authorities that refer to the *document* that you start with. Those listed authorities are called *citing*

---

2. Much of this section is drawn from *Oregon Legal Research* and used with permission.

3. *Gosnell v. Rentokil, Inc.*, 175 F.R.D. 508, 510 (N.D. Ill. 1997).

4. *Golden Eagle Distrib. Corp. v. Burroughs Corp.*, 103 F.R.D. 124, 129 (N.D. Cal. 1984) ("For counsel to have been unaware of those cases means that they did not Shepardize their principal authority....").

5. *Taylor v. Belger Cartage Serv., Inc.*, 102 F.R.D. 172, 180-81 (W.D. Mo. 1984).

6. This portion of the chapter draws from *North Carolina Legal Research*, with permission.

references, citing sources, or *citing documents.*[7] The process of updating involves examining all of the citing authorities that appear potentially relevant to the issues you are researching and seeing how they treat your case.

Shepard's, KeyCite, and BCite provide additional information, called *signals,* for some of the citing authorities, suggesting how they treat your case, the *document.* These signals are typically displayed as color-coded symbols. While these signals may be used to prioritize your research, they should never be solely relied upon in any important research. Each relevant citing authority should be examined. Fortunately, all three systems can help winnow the list of citing authorities both by jurisdiction and by topic or issue of law.

The assignment of signals depends on an editor's interpretation of the issues and outcome in each case. While there are safeguards in place to help prevent mistakes, human error or legitimate difference of opinion is always possible. Additionally, since there are often multiple legal issues in cases, a symbol assigned to a case might only reference a part of the case not relevant to your research. The symbols should only be used to prioritize the order in which the citing authorities are examined. The color-coded symbols for each service are described later in the chapter.

Finally, each service offers ways to filter results and help you narrow your research to the most important authorities for your purpose. Although the location and naming of the filters varies somewhat on each service, the underlying concepts are the same. If you are updating a case you found in your research, and over 300 cases cite to it, it isn't realistic to expect that you will read each of those citing cases in depth. Filters you might use to narrow your results and prioritize your research include filtering by court, which lets you focus on cases from the highest court; filtering by jurisdiction, so that you can limit your results to cases from your own jurisdiction; filtering by date, to see the most recent treatment of your case; and filtering by topic, to explore results that are factually and legally most relevant to the issue you are researching.

IV. Updating Cases Using Shepard's on Lexis Advance

A. Accessing Shepard's

There are a few ways to get started with Shepardizing.

---

7. Since the terminology varies among the three systems, this chapter will refer to them generically as *citing authorities.*

1. Shepardizing a Case Already Displayed on the Screen

Once a case is displayed on the screen, click the "*Shepardize®* this document" link displayed to the right of the case caption. Shepard's will then produce a "Shepard's Report" for your case. Lexis also displays summary information regarding the Shepard's status of the case on the right side of the case display screen; for example, that your case was cited by ten other cases and that it has potentially negative history.

2. Shepardizing a Case Using the Citation

If you have previously conducted some research, found and read a case, and determined it is relevant, you may want to start your next research session by Shepardizing it right away, without having to take the additional step of retrieving the case itself. To do that, enter *shep:* followed immediately by the case citation into the universal search bar on Lexis Advance. So, to Shepardize *Whitehead v. Toyota Motor Corp.*, 897 S.W.2d 684 (Tenn. 1995), enter *shep:897 s.w.2d 684* into the search box to retrieve the Shepard's report.

B. The Shepard's Display

1. Appellate History of a Case

The first screen displayed when you retrieve a Shepard's report is the appellate history of the case. This tab provides both the subsequent and prior history of your case. To view this information in an interactive visual format, click the "Map" button towards the upper right of the screen. With complex cases, the visual presentation can make the flow of litigation more understandable. In the map display, your original case (the *document*) is represented as pin with a rounded top. Other cases are represented as gray or colored boxes, depending on the treatment code assigned to them by a Shepard's editor. If you are unsure as to what a particular symbol represents, click the "Legend" link in the upper left. To see the full text of a case represented in the map, click on the symbol and then select the "Open Document" option.

2. Cases that Cite Your Case

To view all of the cases that cite to your case, click the "Citing Decisions" link. This report lists every case decision in the Lexis Advance system that cites your case. By default, the citing case decisions are ordered first by jurisdiction, then by level of court, and finally by date of decision, with the newest decisions first. So a Tennessee Supreme Court case such as the *Whitehead* case mentioned above, would generate a "Citing Decisions" report with Tennessee Supreme Court cases that cited it listed first, followed by decisions from the Tennessee intermediate courts of appeals. Following that would be federal Sixth Circuit Court of Appeals decisions, and then decisions from District Courts within the Sixth Circuit. You can change the order of the display by using the "Sort by" drop down box towards the upper right.

Selecting the "Analysis" option in the "Sort by" drop down box will bring cases that treat your original case negatively to the top. Lexis Advance editors label each case that cited your case with an analysis label to indicate how it treats your case. These include negative labels such as "criticized by," "questioned by," and "distinguished," positive labels such as "followed by," and neutral labels such as "cited by" and "explained by." In addition, each analysis is categorized and labeled with a colored square that corresponds to the treatment it gave to your original case: warning (red), questioned (orange), caution (yellow), positive (green), and neutral (blue). Figure 6-1 shows an example of the "Citing

Figure 6-1. Shepard's Report

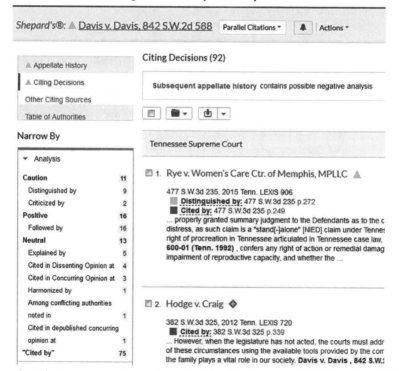

Decisions" tab of a Shepard's Report on Lexis Advance for a Tennessee Supreme Court case, *Davis v. Davis*, 842 S.W.2d 588 (1992).

The link to "Other Citing Sources" provides a list of other materials, such as secondary authorities (law reviews, treatises, legal encyclopedias, etc.), court filings, newspaper articles, and statutory annotations that cite your case. Remember, these lists are not exclusive—as a general rule, they list only sources that are available on Lexis Advance.

Clicking the "Table of Authorities" link will give you a list of the cases cited within your case, along with an analysis status and a status symbol for those cases. Reviewing this information is important—even if your case has not been specifically overturned or reversed, its authoritative weight could be called into question if most of the cases it relies upon have been overturned, criticized, or subject to negative treatment. Conversely, if all of the cases your case cites as authority have been treated positively and remain good law, that can help you to be assured that your case is still good law and viewed favorably as well. Although not a substitute for a thorough analysis of these cases, the Table of Authorities can give a quick indication of the overall status of the authority on which your case relies.

C. The Meaning and Use of the Citator Symbols

Shepard's employs a number of symbols to express the editors' judgment about the value of a cited case so that you may quickly make a reasonable assessment of whether your case is still good law. In addition, the editors weigh the value of each case citing your case and assign symbols to them. These symbols should be used cautiously, and you should read the text of the cases to make your own judgment. The real value in using the symbols is to assist in prioritizing the order in which you read the citing decisions. Table 6-1 lists and defines the Shepard's symbols.

Table 6-1. Shepard's Symbols

Shepard's Symbol	Definition
Red "Stop" Sign	Warning: Shepard's editors have identified strong negative history or treatment of your case. At least part of the case may have been overruled or reversed.
Red Exclamation Point	Warning: Used for statutes, this symbol indicates that your statute has been negatively treated by cases that

	cite it. For example, your statute may have been found to be unconstitutional or void.
Orange "Q"	Questioned: The Shepard's editors have determined that later cases have questioned the continuing validity or precedential value of your case.
Yellow Triangle	Caution: The handling of at least one legal issue in your case has been criticized or distinguished by another case.
Green "+" Sign	Positive Treatment: There is only positive treatment of your case, such as "affirmed" or "followed by."
Blue "A"	Analysis Available: The citing references analyze your case in a neutral manner, such as "explained."
Blue "I"	Citation Information Available: later cases merely cite your case, without giving it any definitive treatment.

You may see symbols in several places in the Shepard's report. The most important symbol is the one at the top of the screen, next to the name of your case. Hover your cursor over the symbol for a quick reminder of its meaning. Alternatively, you can scroll to the bottom of the screen and click on the "Legend" button on the right to see all of the symbols and their meanings. Citing cases or references may also have symbols next to them. These symbols often prove confusing to new legal researchers. Figure 6-2 shows an example of a Shepard's Report for the case *State v. Smith*, 834 S.W.2d 915 (Tenn. 1992).

Many people who are new to legal research will look at the citing references and jump to the conclusion that the red stop sign next to *State v. White* indicates that *State v. White* overruled or reversed *State v. Smith*. In fact, the red stop sign next to *State v. White* means that *State v. White* was later overruled or reversed. It has nothing to do with how *State v. White* treated *State v. Smith*. In that regard, *White* distinguished *Smith* on some grounds but did not overrule or reverse it. You can tell that by the line "Distinguished by:" just underneath the citation for *White*.

Knowing how citing cases such as *White* have been treated can be important, especially if they have, like *White*, been overruled or reversed. Generally, however, you are mostly interested in the symbol that the Shepard's editors applied to your case at the top of the screen. The significance of these two differently placed symbols should not be confused.

Figure 6-2. Shepard's Report for *State v. Smith*

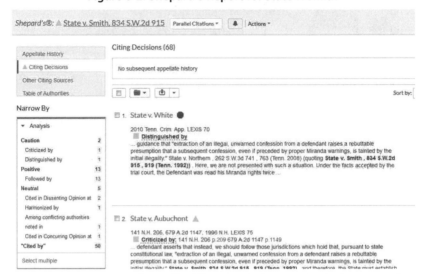

D. Narrowing the Citing Decisions and Other Citing References

For cases that have been frequently cited and display a lengthy citation report, it may be useful to limit the type of information included in the report. One extreme example is *Roe v. Wade*, 410 U.S. 113 (1973). With over 18,000 citing cases and other references on Lexis Advance, the only reasonable way of beginning to analyze them is to narrow your results strictly.

Shepard's offers several ways to narrow the results. In this instance, if you are most interested in how later cases have treated *Roe* (rather than, for example, how scholarly commentators have discussed *Roe*), of course your first step is to choose "Citing Decisions" rather than "Other Citing Sources." That narrows your field down to over 4,000 cases that have cited *Roe*. That is a much smaller group, but it will still need significant filtering. Once you have limited your Shepard's results to citing decisions, you can further narrow your results by type of analysis (did the citing case treat *Roe* negatively or positively?), by jurisdiction/court, by the depth of discussion of *Roe* within the citing case, by the headnote assigned by Lexis editors, by keyword, and by date. Any filters that can be applied to your case will appear on the left side of the report.

It is also possible to search for terms within all of the cases (or other citing references) listed on the Shepard's report. You can get very specific with your search terms, which can be helpful if you are looking for cases that address a narrow issue of law, or that fit a tight fact pattern.

The "Timeline" section allows you to narrow the results to a particular date and displays a graph of how often your case has been cited over time. This filter is useful if, for example, you are looking for very recent cases. The graph provides a quick visual indication of how important your case has been at various times. If it was cited frequently fifty years ago but is rarely cited now, you might try to find a case that seems to be more highly regarded by recent courts, or to look even more carefully at whether your case has been in some way called into question or criticized in recent years.

E. Analyzing the Citing Sources' Treatment of Your Case

Although the editors provide eye-catching symbols signifying positive and potentially negative treatment of your case, it is your responsibility to interpret how the citing sources affect your case. The essence of updating with citators is the application of your professional judgment to the treatment given to your case by the citing sources.

Clicking on the name of a citing source in your results links you to the relevant part of that case (or other source) that refers to your case. If the pinpointed information you are linked to seems relevant, be sure to read the entire document so that you understand the pinpointed information in context.

You may also find that many cases cite your case for a point of law you are not researching. These cases are not relevant to your inquiry and can safely be excluded from further careful reading. Also, a number of citing cases may simply cite your case without ascribing any meaning or value to it. These citing cases can generally be disregarded.

Other benefits may come from the time and effort spent updating cases. For example, one of the cases citing your case may actually be more legally or factually on-target to support your claim or defense. A citing case might raise additional relevant issues you had yet to consider. Because of these research benefits, you would be wise to update cases throughout the research process, rather than waiting until the end of your research.

V. Updating Cases Using KeyCite on Westlaw

A. Accessing KeyCite

When a case (or other document) is displayed on Westlaw, KeyCite information is automatically provided along the top of the case in tabs. What is included in those KeyCite tabs is discussed in more detail in Part V. B., below.

Figure 6-3 provides an example of how a Tennessee case, *Clinard v. Pennington*, 438 S.W.2d 748 (Tenn. Ct. App. 1974), and its KeyCite tabs, are displayed on Westlaw.

The KeyCite status flag is displayed next to the case name. For cases that have significant negative treatment, a brief summary of that treatment is provided just below the KeyCite tabs. In the *Clinard* case shown in Figure 6-3, there is a red flag next to the case name in the upper left of the screen display, and the red flag is repeated just above the case caption with the notation, "Overruled by Teeters v. Currey."

If you already have a case citation and want to access its KeyCite tabs directly without first retrieving the full text of the opinion, type *kc* or *keycite* followed by the citation into the main search bar. For example, *kc 241 sw2d 595* will take you directly to the KeyCite tabs for the case *Aetna Life Insurance Co. v. Bidwell*, 241 S.W.2d 595 (Tenn. 1951).

Figure 6-3 Case and KeyCite Tabs on Westlaw

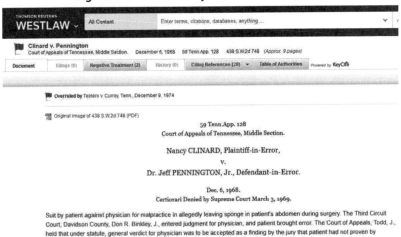

Source: Westlaw, image reprinted with permission of West, a Thomson Reuters business.

B. The KeyCite Tabs

The "History" tab provides the direct history of your case, to the extent that it is recorded on Westlaw. This direct history includes, for example, whether your case reversed or remanded a lower court's ruling, or whether your case was appealed and its disposition on appeal. This information is presented in both a list and flow chart form. Especially when your case was part of complex litigation, the flow chart can help you understand the procedural history of the case. The case names in both the list and the flow chart are linked to the full text of the decisions, when they are available on Westlaw.

The "Negative Treatment" tab first presents any negative direct history, meaning your case later went up to the next level of appellate court and was reversed. After negative direct history comes the more general category of negative citing references: citing cases that overrule, criticize, decline to extend, distinguish, modify, or call into doubt your case. The cases in the "Negative Treatment" tab are organized by the way they treat your case: all cases that "call into doubt" your case are grouped together, as are all cases that "decline to extend" your case, and so on. At least theoretically, the "most negative" type of treatment is listed first, followed by the treatment with the next degree of negativity, all the way through. However, keep in mind that this determination is subjective, and you should make your own judgment. After type of treatment, negative cases are sorted by jurisdiction and then in reverse chronological order. You cannot re-sort or filter the order of the cases in this tab. To explore your filtering and sorting options, click over to the "Citing References" tab.

The "Citing References" tab lists all the cases and other authorities that cite your case. The default order of these results places the cases that have most in-depth discussion of your case at the top of the list. You can confirm this by looking at the "Depth" column in the results table. Cases with four green squares in the "Depth" column *examined* your case (extended discussion of your case). Three green squares means the citing case *discussed* your case (substantial discussion of your case), two green squares means the citing case *cited* your case (some discussion of your case) one on green square means the citing case *mentioned* your case (a brief reference with no real discussion). If there are multiple citing cases that give the same depth of treatment to your case, the citing cases within that group that treat your case most negatively will be listed first.

Other columns in the "Citing References" tab tell you the exact treatment given to your case, the date the citing case was decided, and the headnotes (specific topics and issues) from your case that are referenced or implicated by the citing case. You can change the ordering of the citing cases by using the

"Sort By" box above the table of results or by clicking on the headings of the "Depth" and "Date" columns.

The "Citing References" tab also lets you see which law review articles, legal treatises, and court filings have cited your case. Use the filters on the left side of the "Citing References" page to view secondary sources, administrative decisions, or other types of sources that have cited your case.

The "Table of Authorities" tab lists all of the cases that are cited by your case. Each case in the table has a status flag next to it, which indicates how it was treated by later cases. Inspecting the table of authorities can give you an indication of the overall status of the cases upon which your case relies. Even if your case has not been treated negatively, you would want to seriously consider the weight you would place on your case if every case it relies upon for a particular point of law has been criticized or overruled.

C. The Meaning and Use of KeyCite Status Flags

KeyCite uses colored flags to denote how cases have been treated by subsequent cases and statutes, focusing on possible negative treatment. If West editors have determined that a case has definite or possible negative treatment, for any of the points of law it decided, it will have a red or yellow flag near the case name. Although you should not rely on the status flag as authoritative, this quick signal of the strength of a case can be useful for prioritizing your research. A red flag indicates that a case is no longer good law for at least one of the points of law it decided, while a yellow flag indicates that the case has some negative history but it has not been reversed or overturned. You may also occasionally see a blue-and-white striped flag, which indicates that a case is on appeal with either an intermediate federal appellate court or the United States Supreme Court.

D. Limiting the KeyCite Results

When a case has been cited by many other cases, it may not be realistic to attempt to review each citing case. Important cases that were decided decades ago could have tens of thousands of citing authorities. *Miranda v. Arizona* has been cited by over 58,000 cases, not to mention over 55,000 other authorities, such as law review articles and appellate briefs. Due to time constraints, a best practice would be to use KeyCite to assist in selecting and prioritizing the cases to be reviewed. For most research scenarios, cases suggesting negative treatment should be reviewed first. KeyCite filters can limit the citing references to those that are most relevant to your research.

When viewing the "Citing References" tab, the available filters will be shown on the left side of the page. This list of filters will be different depending on the type of citing references you are reviewing. For example, if no cases cite your case, that filter will not appear in the left margin. If only Tennessee cases cite your case, only that state will be listed under the "Jurisdiction" filter.

Potential filters for cases include jurisdiction, date, headnote topic, treatment status, and reported status (so that you can choose to filter out unpublished cases that cite to your case). You can also use the search box in the left filter column to search for key words within the citing sources. To use more than one filter, click on "Select Multiple Filters."

The citing cases' jurisdiction filter is quite useful, for example, when researching a federal issue where you might only be interested in citing cases from the Sixth Circuit Court of Appeals or federal trial level decisions from Tennessee.

Another very useful filter for KeyCite Citing References involves the headnotes from your case. Most issues decide points of law on a range of issues, and typically researchers are interested in only one issue, or group of related issues, from a case. For example, the *Clinard v. Pennington* case depicted in Figure 6-3 has headnotes with several assigned West topics, including Appeal & Error, Limitation of Actions, Health, and Trial. If you are planning to use *Clinard* strictly for the statute of limitations ruling, you can scroll down to the "Headnote Topics" filter and check the box next to "Limitation of Actions." This filter will remove the citing cases that only deal with non-relevant topics such as Health and Trial from your KeyCite results.

As discussed above, KeyCite analyzes the depth of treatment each citing case provides your case. The depth of treatment limitation is useful when you have a great number of citing cases and would find it most helpful to view those cases that discuss your case in the most depth.

E. Analyzing the Citing Cases' Treatment of Your Case

Again, there is no substitute for examining the cases yourself. Certainly all the cases relied upon from the KeyCite results should be closely examined. The legal issues from each of those cases should be understood within the entire context of that case and not read in isolation.

VI. Updating Cases Using BCite on Bloomberg Law

As a relative newcomer to the legal market, Bloomberg Law's BCite is the newest citator product. It was developed in the 2000s, when Bloomberg Law decided to add an editorially created citator to its product.

When viewing a case on Bloomberg Law, the BCite symbol appears next to the case name to indicate the general status of the case. Details appear on the right column under the "BCite Analysis" heading and in the tabs across the top of the document. Figure 6-4 shows the case *Eckler v. Allen*, 231 S.W.3d 379 (Tenn. Ct. App. 2007) as it is displayed in Bloomberg Law, with BCite tabs across the top of the case display and the BCite Analysis pane on the right.

Your case's prior and subsequent history can be viewed by clicking the "Direct History" link or tab. All of the cases citing your case, along with a breakdown by treatment indicator (such as positive, distinguished, or criticized) are shown in the "Case Analysis" link or tab. See Table 6-2 for a list of the BCite indicators.

Figure 6-4. Case with BCite Analysis on Bloomberg Law

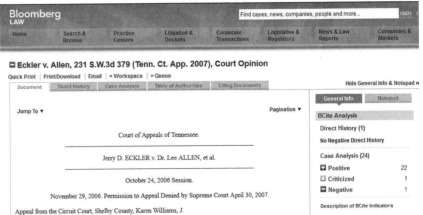

Table 6-2. BCite Treatment Indicators

BCite Symbol   Description

Green with Plus Sign	Positive: one or more courts cite this case with approval.
Gray with Plus Sign	No courts have cited this case.
Blue with Slash	Distinguished: one or more courts cited this case and distinguished it based on law or facts.
Yellow with Triangle	Caution: case has been modified, clarified, amended, or criticized.
Orange with Circle	Superseded by statute: one or more courts have noted that the case has been superseded by an intervening statute or regulation.
Red with Horizontal Bar	Negative: case has been reversed, vacated, depublished, or overruled wholly or in part.

To view all of the cases that cite your case, click the "Case Analysis" link or tab. By default, this list is in chronological order, but can be changed to sort by "Citation Frequency" (most-cited cases listed first), "Citing Case Analysis" (cases that treat your case most negatively will be listed first), or by court. BCite also offers a number of filters that can be used to limit the results: analysis, citing case status, citation frequency, court, judge, and date. The "Citing Case Analysis" filter allows you to see cases that have treated your case in a particular way, such as "Followed" or "Criticized." The "Citing Case Status" filter allows you to see cases that have received a particular type of treatment of their own, such as cases that have received positive treatment, or cases that have received negative treatment. Note that there is no way to filter the results by topic on this tab. There is a topic filter for cases, though, on the "Citing Documents" tab.

The "Citing Documents" tab provides a list of all documents (not just cases) on Bloomberg Law that cite your case. You can filter the results by content type—court opinions, law reviews, pleadings, books and treatises, and so on, as well as by date. Once you have filtered by content type, additional filters may be available. For example, if you filter to court opinions, you can then filter by topic. If you filter to law review articles, you can then filter to a particular publication.

The "Table of Authorities" tab lists the cases cited within your case and indicates how these cases were treated by your case as well as the general status symbol for each case, quickly suggesting the overall status of the authority on which your case relies.

VII. Updating Cases Using Authority Check on Fastcase

Members of the Tennessee Bar Association are provided free access to the online research service Fastcase as part of their bar membership. The Fastcase subscription includes constitutions, statutes, regulations, and court opinions from all fifty states and the federal government. The Authority Check feature on Fastcase functions similarly to a citator service. Authority Check generates a list of cases which have cited your case. Authority Check is fully automated, meaning the computer algorithm searches the text of court opinions for citations that match your case's citation. There is no human input in terms of gathering or analyzing later citing cases and how they treat your case. This puts more of the onus on you to carefully review and analyze the citing cases.

When you run a case search on Fastcase, your results table will include a column on the right for Authority Check, quickly telling you how many cases (and other authorities on Fastcase) have cited your case. You can use this column to sort your results, so that the most-cited cases are on the top. You can access the Authority Check results directly from your search by clicking the number listed in the Authority Check column. This will take you to the Authority Check report. At the top of the report is a graphical timeline showing when, and by what courts, your case has been cited. Next to the timeline is a summary of the citations your case has received. Beneath the timeline are lists of cases and law review articles that have cited your case. The list of cases includes a brief excerpt from each case, showing your cited case in context.

Although Authority Check does not provide case analysis, and disclaimers with the service state that it "does not include editorial information telling you whether your case is still good law," it does use a computer algorithm to try to identify cases that have received negative treatment. If the algorithm (the charmingly named "Bad Law Bot") identifies such a case, you will see a red flag next to the case name. However, the algorithm is very limited in what it looks for. The presence of a red flag should definitely be noted, but the absence of a red flag does not always mean that a case is still good law. Figure 6-5 shows the Authority Check report for *Hannan v. Alltel Publishing Co.*, a Tennessee Supreme Court case that was recently overruled.

Figure 6-5. Authority Check Report from Fastcase

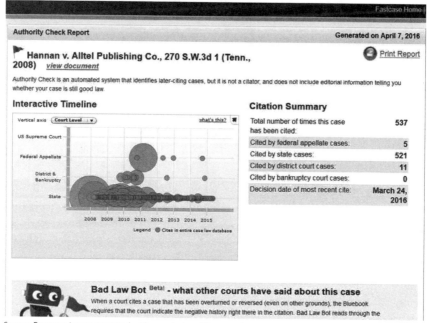

Source: Fastcase. Image reprinted with permission of Fastcase, Inc.

VIII. Updating Cases on Google Scholar

Although using free Internet resources for case law research is fraught with peril, many attorneys may choose to at least start their research in free resources, particularly Google Scholar. After running a search in Google Scholar's case law database, you will see each case in the results list includes a link under the case name indicating how many cases and other authorities have cited that case ("Cited by [number]"). In addition, there will be a "How cited" link that allows you to jump to a list of cases that gives more detail of how your case has been cited. If your case has been quoted by other cases, those quotes will be included at the top of the "How cited" report. In addition, a table of citations on the right side of the page uses blue bars to show in how much depth your case was treated by the citing cases. Three blue bars means your case was discussed in depth, while zero blue bars means the case was merely cited with no further discussion. Figure 6-6 shows the "How cited" report for the Tennessee Supreme Court case *Landers v. Jones*, 872 S.W.2d 674 (Tenn. 1994).

Figure 6-6. Google Scholar "How Cited" Report

Landers v. Jones, 872 SW 2d 674 - Tenn: Supreme Court 1994   Google Scholar

Read   How cited   Search

How this document has been cited	Cited by
" The existence of subject matter jurisdiction depends on the nature of the cause of action and the relief sought. **"** - in MIDWESTERN GAS TRANSMISSION COMPANY v. Smith, 2006 and 63 similar citations	☰ Shaw v. Shaw Tenn: Court of Appeals 2011
" "Subject matter jurisdiction concerns the authority of a particular court to hear a particular controversy." **"** - in Bullard v. TURNEY CENTER DISCIPLINARY BOARD, 2012 and 26 similar citations	☰ PEK v. JM 52 SW 3d 653 - Tenn: Court of Appeals, Middle Section 2001
" "In order to adjudicate a claim, a court must possess both subject matter jurisdiction and personal jurisdiction." **"** - in State v. O'NEAL, 2008 and 6 similar citations	☰ In re Frumkin 912 SW 2d 138 - Tenn: Court of Appeals, Eastern Section 1995
" The Court held that such a motion did not constitute a general appearance, saying "waiver occurs only if there is no objection to personal jurisdiction in the first filing, either a Rule 12 motion or an answer." **"** - in PEK v. JM, 2001 and 4 similar citations	☰ NEWGATE RECOVERY, LLC v. HOLROB-HARVEY ROAD, LLC Tenn: Court of Appeals 2014

Source: Google Scholar. Google and the Google logo are registered trademarks of Google Inc., used with permission.

Keep in mind when using these Google Scholar citation features that no humans curate the results. Instead, computer algorithms seek the citation of your case in later documents and assess how much language the citing case (or article) draws from your cited case. "How cited" and "Cited by" will not tell you whether a case has been overruled, reversed, criticized, or otherwise called into question.

In the "Cited by" list, filters on the left side of the page allow you to narrow to a particular jurisdiction or court or a specific time range. You can also use a link on the left to switch the result order from relevance ranking to chronological ranking. You can search within your results by using the search bar at the top of the screen and checking the "Search within citing articles" box underneath the name of the case you are researching. Finally, a link on the left side of the page lets you create an email alert to be notified any time a new case or article cites your case.

IX. Updating Statutes

State and federal statutes may be updated using either Shepard's or KeyCite. Bloomberg Law's BCite and Fastcase's Authority Check do not cover statutes at this time. Because statutes are different from cases in the way they are created and updated, the results from KeyCite and Shepard's are different for statutes than they are for cases. However, the process of updating statutes is similar to the process for updating cases.

A. Using Shepard's on Lexis Advance to Update Statutes

On Lexis Advance, click the "*Shepardize®* this document" link on the right side of the page. You may also see graphical symbols indicating the status of the statute. Shepard's statute presentation is similar to its case presentation. It defaults to the "Citing Decisions" tab, which has the same filtering and sorting options as discussed with respect to Shepard's case citation results. The "Other Citing Sources" tab provides links to constitutions, annotated codes, secondary authorities, and court filings that cite your statute. The "Legislative History" tab links to session laws that created or amended the statute, as well as to any pending legislation that would affect the statute if passed.

Compared to its citation reports for cases, Shepard's does not provide as many symbols for statutes. Many of the editorial judgments concerning statutes are spelled out, rather than summarized with a graphical symbol. Shepard's uses a red exclamation point for legislative or judicial changes affecting the statute. A yellow exclamation point suggests pending legislation that would affect the statute if enacted into law.

B. Using KeyCite to Update Statutes

On Westlaw, KeyCite tabs will be displayed across the top of the statute. Just as with case opinions, these tabs allow you to access information on the status and treatment of the statute. The "History" tab provides summaries of how the statute has changed over time and links to prior versions of the statute and legislative history materials, to the extent they are available on Westlaw. The "Citing References" tab includes links to cases and secondary authorities, such as *American Law Reports* and *Tennessee Practice*, that cite to your statute. The "Context & Analysis" tab lists references to related statutes and regulations, as well as to secondary authorities selected by the West editors as being particularly relevant.

Westlaw may also place a red or yellow flag on a statute to indicate possible issues with its currency and effectiveness. A red flag means that the statute has been amended by a recently passed law, repealed, superseded, held unconstitutional, or preempted in whole or in part. A yellow flag means a statute has been recently re-numbered, that there is pending legislation that, if passed, would affect the statute, that the statute was limited on constitutional or preemption grounds or its validity otherwise questioned by a court, or that a prior version of the statute was treated negatively by a court.

C. Targeting Statutory Updates

When using Shepard's, you can choose to focus on the narrowest section of the relevant code in order to retrieve the most targeted results with the fewest irrelevant entries, or use a citation higher in the statutory hierarchy to receive broader, more comprehensive results. Say that you are researching case law treatment of Tenn. Code Ann. § 39-13-202(a)(3), which specifically deals with first degree murder committed by a bomb or explosive device. When you pull up the Shepard's Report for the main statutory section, 39-13-202, you will find almost 2,000 cases have cited that statute. However, as you glance over the citing cases, you will see that the vast majority have nothing to do with the specific subsection (a)(3). To target your Shepard's Report just to the subsection you are researching, click the "Subsection Reports" link, then scroll down to find just the cases that refer to (a)(3): in this instance, a much more manageable nineteen case citations.

KeyCite has a similar targeting function, but it currently is only available for some federal statutes. If you are KeyCiting a federal statute, after navigating to the "Citing References" tab, you may see a "Subsections" filter on the left side of the page, allowing you to narrow the results to just the subsection you are researching. Unfortunately, there is no such filter available for state statutes.

X. Updating Other Legal Authorities

In addition to cases and statutes, other authorities may be updated using KeyCite and Shepard's, although coverage varies. For instance, you can KeyCite Tennessee administrative regulations, but you cannot Shepardize them. Tennessee court rules may be updated on either service, and both Shepard's and KeyCite will generate reports showing what authorities have cited to secondary authorities such as law reviews or treatises. Additional authorities such as attorney general opinions and jury instructions may also be "updateable," depending on which service you are using.

Chapter 7

Researching Secondary Authorities

I. Introduction[1]

Law professors, legal experts, editorial staff of legal publishing companies, and even law students write commentary about the law. This commentary is considered to be secondary to the law itself, which is written by legislatures, courts, and administrative agencies. Although there are levels of persuasiveness among secondary authorities, none of them provides mandatory authority that must be followed in any jurisdiction. However, secondary authorities are an important component in the process of finding and understanding primary law.

A. The Role of Secondary Authorities in the Legal Research Process

The savvy researcher quickly learns how to use secondary authorities in almost any legal research project, both to learn about the law and to find citations to primary authority. Secondary authorities provide an excellent starting point for research, whether using print or online sources. Particularly when researching an unfamiliar area of law, a few minutes spent reviewing an appropriate secondary authority provides the level of background information that you need to enhance your understanding of the legal issues involved in a research project. This understanding greatly improves your research process by (1) enabling you to select more relevant research terms when searching databases, indexes, or digests; (2) providing direct citations to relevant primary authority; and (3) facilitating a faster, deeper, and more efficient recognition and understanding of the primary law retrieved in the research process.

---

1. This part of the chapter draws from *North Carolina Legal Research*, with permission.

B. Types of Secondary Authorities

Legal encyclopedias, legal treatises, law reviews or journals, *American Law Reports* annotations, and Restatements of the Law are the five traditional types of secondary authority. Each of these authorities provides a unique view of law and may have different purposes throughout the research process. These five secondary authorities will be addressed in turn to begin this chapter. Many other secondary authorities might be categorized as practice materials; they are covered later in the chapter. These materials include continuing legal education materials, legal forms, model jury instructions, uniform laws, and law-related blogs. The chapter concludes with a brief discussion of choosing appropriate types of secondary authorities for your particular research issue.

II. Traditional Secondary Authorities

A. Legal Encyclopedias

The two main national legal encyclopedias are *American Jurisprudence* and *Corpus Juris Secundum*. Many states have their own encyclopedias. Tennessee's is *Tennessee Jurisprudence*. Legal encyclopedias are one of the most basic of the secondary authorities and, if available, are often most useful as a beginning point for legal research. Legal encyclopedias are organized the in same way that general encyclopedias such as *Encyclopedia Britannica* are. Information is organized into topics, and the topics are arranged in alphabetical order in a multi-volume encyclopedia set.

1. Researching Legal Encyclopedias in Print

The spine of each of the encyclopedia volumes shows the alphabetic range of topics included in that volume. For example, the topic "Contracts" would be included in a volume with Constitutional Law—Correctional Law on the spine. The spine will not list each and every topic included in the volume. It will just show the alphabetic range of topics.

To use an encyclopedia, review its softbound index volumes, usually shelved at the end of the set, for your research terms. The references will include both an abbreviated word or phrase—the topic—and a section number.[2] For example, imagine you are researching what types of damage are covered under automobile collision insurance. You would go to the index, look up Automobile

---

2. Do not confuse the section number with a volume or page number.

Insurance → Collision → Types of Damage, Generally, and see a reference to "Auto Ins § 131."

Next, find the volume with the Automobile Insurance topic. But instead of turning directly to section 131 in that topic, go to the beginning of the topic and find its table of contents. Skim the table of contents and other basic introductory material there for an overview and general information. This small extra step will help you gain context and gather ideas for potential further research. Then turn to section 131 and read the text there.

The text of most encyclopedia entries is cursory because the goal of the writers is to summarize the law rather than to analyze it in great depth. Entries in national encyclopedias will identify major variations that exist between different jurisdictions, but they do not attempt to resolve differences or recommend improvements in the law.

The footnotes that accompany the text in an encyclopedia are often just as helpful as the text, if not more so. The footnotes will usually cite directly to primary authorities, such as case opinions and statutes, that support the commentary in the discussion. Because finding and citing primary authorities is almost always the ultimate goal of any legal researcher, using these footnotes as a springboard to further research in primary authorities is often an efficient way to begin your research.

In *Tennessee Jurisprudence*, those footnotes will generally refer to Tennessee authorities that uphold and apply the principles discussed in the text. In a national encyclopedia, the citations to authorities could be from any, or many, states. You can still use those citations to find Tennessee cases addressing the same principles, though. One way to do this is to look up the cases from another jurisdiction in a West reporter or on Westlaw, note the most relevant West topic and key number, and then use the topic and key number to locate similar Tennessee cases. As with virtually all other print-based legal research, you must check the pocket parts of encyclopedias to find references to the most recent authorities and commentary.

2. *Tennessee Jurisprudence*

Tennessee Jurisprudence provides textual analysis of more than 400 subjects with citations to Tennessee statutes and rules, case law, and law review articles. On Lexis Advance, you can access *Tennessee Jurisprudence* by typing *Tennessee Jurisprudence* into the main search bar. You will be given the option to either search the encyclopedia ("add as search filter") or browse it by linking to the online Table of Contents. *Tennessee Jurisprudence* is not available on Westlaw or on Bloomberg Law.

3. *American Jurisprudence 2d*

American Jurisprudence 2d ("Am. Jur.") is a broad, encyclopedic treatment of American law covering state and federal law, civil and criminal law, and procedural and substantive law. The encyclopedia is maintained and updated by an editorial staff. Am. Jur. has traditionally excelled at covering federal law issues, although it certainly covers state law as well.

Am. Jur. is available on Westlaw by simply entering *amjur* or *American Jurisprudence* in the universal search bar. Although keyword searching the encyclopedia's full text often retrieves too many irrelevant passages, a nifty feature of the database is the ability to browse the entire table of contents. You may browse the titles and use them as a menu by continuing to select relevant topic and subtopic headings until you reach the encyclopedia text. You can also access the index to Am. Jur. on Westlaw. You will find the link to it on the right hand side of the main Am. Jur. page, in the "Tools and Resources" column. The Westlaw version of Am. Jur. is typically updated every few months.

Am. Jur. is also available to search or browse on Lexis Advance. Again, just type *American Jurisprudence* or *amjur* into the universal search bar. Because Am. Jur. is currently being published by West, Am. Jur. on Lexis Advance may only be at least as current as the latest pocket part for the print encyclopedia. The Am. Jur. index is not available on Lexis Advance. Am. Jur. is not available at all on Bloomberg Law.

4. *Corpus Juris Secundum*

Corpus Juris Secundum ("CJS") is another broad legal encyclopedia attempting to comprehensively describe American law by covering all state and federal legal topics. One distinction of CJS is the availability of "black letter" summaries of general rules of law throughout the text. CJS has traditionally been noted for its coverage of state law and exhaustive citations to cases.

CJS is available as a database on Westlaw by typing *CJS* in the universal search bar. The table of contents feature is available for CJS as well as the ability to search the full text with keywords or natural language. CJS is not available on Lexis Advance or on Bloomberg Law.

B. Treatises

A "treatise" is a book on a particular topic in the law, such as environmental law or federal civil procedure. These include a wide variety of types of books, such as nutshells, hornbooks, and professional treatises. All of these books share the purpose of covering a single legal topic. They may also narrow their focus by exclusively covering a single jurisdiction, such as Tennessee. A book on a legal topic can provide a deeper discussion and more relevant references than might be found in an encyclopedia entry. The various types of books are distinguished from each other by their respective depth of coverage and the audience to whom they are directed. They may be broadly focused, providing an excellent overview of a topic, or narrowly focused for in-depth analysis. A legal treatise exists for nearly every imaginable legal subject. The value of the information depends upon several factors, including the reputation and knowledge of the author, how up-to-date the book is, and the skill and expertise of the editors or publishers.

1. Nutshells

One of the most basic series of treatises is the "Nutshell" series published by West. There are hundreds of Nutshells, such as *Contracts in a Nutshell* and *Criminal Law in a Nutshell*. They tend to be most frequently used by law students and members of the general public seeking an introduction to a particular area of law. Nutshells are usually authored by law professors, respected for their knowledge in a particular legal field. They typically do not provide citations to primary law, but rather provide a broad overview of a legal topic, giving a researcher the main ideas and how they may be understood in the broadest context. Nutshells are national in scope and would rarely, if ever, provide state-specific information about Tennessee.

To find a Nutshell in your library, start by doing a key word search in the library catalog using a word or two that might be in the title combined with the word *nutshell*. Because the books in the Nutshell series all contain the word *nutshell* in the title (such as *Criminal Procedure in a Nutshell*), this type of search should retrieve a Nutshell on the subject you are studying if it is in the library's collection.

Many academic law libraries also provide access to Nutshells online, via the West Academic Study Aids database. If you are a law student and are unsure as to whether your law library provides this online access, check with one of your reference librarians. Nutshells are not available on Westlaw, Lexis Advance, or Bloomberg Law.

2. Hornbooks

Hornbooks, another category of treatises, are more detailed in description and explanation of an area of law than a Nutshell, although often still contained in one volume. They are also usually national in scope and tend to provide the enduring principles of the law in some detail, including limited citations to important statutes or seminal cases from a few jurisdictions in the United States. Hornbooks, like Nutshells, are typically written on topics that correspond to law school courses or general areas of legal academic inquiry.

Sometimes hornbooks are authored by law professors who have also authored a Nutshell on the same topic. Examples include Cox and Hazen's *Business Organizations Law*, Perillo's *Contracts*, and Dobbs' *The Law of Torts*. Although these titles are all from West's Hornbook series, any book that meets the description above is categorized generically as a hornbook, and many legal publishers provide multiple hornbook series for use by students, professors, and other legal researchers. Carolina Academic Press's "Mastering" series and "Understanding" series both provide a broad overview of a legal subject with limited citations to legal authority and are popular hornbooks for law students.

Print hornbooks are typically updated either by pocket parts or by regularly issuing new editions of the hornbook.

Whether hornbooks are available online varies considerably, depending on the title, series, and publisher. Some hornbook series are available as part of separate ebook subscription packages. It is unusual to find them on Westlaw, Lexis Advance, or Bloomberg Law.

3. Professional Treatises

Professional treatises or "looseleafs"[3] are much more detailed, typically published in multi-volume sets and usually extensively footnoted with citations. These treatises provide comprehensive description of legal areas in fine detail. Because they often delve beyond the enduring principles and also describe the more rapidly developing areas of law, they are updated more often. Serving as practice guides for attorneys and research compendia for academics, a few such works are so widely used and highly thought of that they are cited and referenced almost as if they were mandatory authorities. These works are often referred to in practice just by the name of the author or by a shortened title, which may be confusing for a new legal researcher. Examples include *McCormick on Evidence*, *Nimmer on Copyright*, *Chisum on Patents*, and *Bogert on*

---

3. In their print versions, these works are usually published in three-ring binders with looseleaf pages. New pages are shipped to the libraries for frequent updating. The new pages are inserted and outdated pages removed, so that researchers can read the most up-to-date information without having to skip back and forth between the main text of the volume and a pocket part or separate supplement.

Trusts. Many professional treatises are available on either Westlaw or Lexis Advance, depending on the publisher.

4. Tennessee Treatises

A number of treatises focus on Tennessee law. These materials are extremely valuable and highly recommended because they are written by legal experts, describe the law in Tennessee, and cite Tennessee authorities. Examples of well known works in Tennessee include *Pritchard on the Law of Wills and Administration of Estates: Embracing the Law and Practice in Tennessee* (often simply called "Pritchard"), *Richards on Tennessee Family Law*, *Gibson's Suits in Chancery*, and Cohen et al.'s *Tennessee Law of Evidence*.[4]

5. Finding Treatises

Although using treatises is relatively easy, finding them may be challenging. A seasoned researcher quickly learns the names of the treatise titles relevant to her field of research; however, when researching an unfamiliar area, locating relevant and authoritative treatises may be difficult. The easiest approach is to ask someone who regularly researches or practices in the area. For example, in law school, ask a reference librarian or a faculty member. In a law firm, a librarian or an associate who researches in an area would be a good choice. You also might browse your library collection or find an online research guide dedicated to your topic or jurisdiction.

Because treatises are based upon the author's hard-earned knowledge and because a great deal of work is involved in the preparation and development of treatises, they are not available for free on the Internet. Because of their value, however, some of them are available online through commercial services such as Westlaw, Lexis Advance, and Bloomberg Law. Browsing the secondary authorities area of these online services should lead you to the individual works, even when you do not know the treatise title.

Another way to find treatises on commercial research services is to explore "Practice Area" links for a work on a particular subject. You might also want to focus on finding treatises for your jurisdiction. To find Tennessee treatises on Westlaw, click on the "State Materials" tab, then "Tennessee," then "All Secondary Resources," and then "All Texts and Treatises." On Lexis Advance, click the "State" tab, then "Tennessee," and then "All Tennessee Treatises, Practice

---

4. Together these treatises have been cited by Tennessee appellate courts over 1100 times since 2000.

Guides, and Jurisprudence." Bloomberg Law does not have any Tennessee-specific treatises at this time.

Remember that you may have access to ebook versions of these treatises through West Academic Study Aids, LexisNexis eBooks, or other ebook collections. Often, these titles will be included by default when you do a search on your law library's catalog, but you may want to check with a reference librarian to make sure you are looking in all available sources and collections.

Once located, either in print or online, treatises are usually best approached using the index or table of contents to find the information needed. Many of the treatises online include a browsable table of contents and an index with hyperlinks to the main text. However, if you are researching online and are not finding what you need with the index or table of contents, try a text search using search terms related to your issue to locate portions of the treatise that may be relevant.

C. Legal Periodicals

The category of "legal periodicals" encompasses many different publications. Predominantly, researchers think of legal periodicals as law reviews and journals published by law schools. Almost all of the 205 ABA-approved law schools publish at least one journal and many publish two or more. Law students at these institutions select and edit the articles for publication. Some of the journals publish articles on any subject while others focus on particular legal subjects, such as banking law or the First Amendment.

Typically, the featured articles are written by law professors, judges, attorneys, and law students and are heavily footnoted by the authors. The articles may describe the law but, more importantly, often analyze, compare, and critique the law. Without the constraints of representing a client's interests or deciding a particular case, an author is able to explore whether the laws currently in force are the best legal rules and to propose changes in the law. These articles may also identify weaknesses or new trends in the law that might be relevant to a client's situation.

When articles are focused on a relevant topic, the references to primary authorities may provide extremely important research information that can save hours of independent work. When dealing with cutting-edge legal issues, however, you might not find much, or any, primary authority on point because that authority might not exist. Law review articles may be especially persuasive then. They will also point to persuasive primary authorities that support your arguments because they uphold analogous or related principles of law.

The law schools in Tennessee—the University of Tennessee, University of Memphis, Vanderbilt University, Belmont University, and Lincoln Memorial University—produce a number of law journals. Some of the journals specifically address Tennessee law, but most do not. Some of the journals are subject specific, such as the *Mental Health Law & Policy Journal*, published at the Cecil B. Humphreys School of Law at the University of Memphis, and the *Vanderbilt Journal of Entertainment & Technology Law*. Law journals from the state's law schools are often excellent secondary sources for relevant legal analysis and critique. Law journals from outside of Tennessee may also publish articles useful to Tennessee researchers.

1. Free Access on the Internet

Many academic law journals make the full text of recent issues freely available on the Internet. A few journals post substantial archives of journal issues on their websites. Although this is a free source when available, the quantity and variety of material posted has typically been inconsistent and irregular enough to make it unreliable as a first choice when researching legal journals. Using a journal's website may, however, be a good approach for a researcher seeking a specific, recent article.

An alternative to searching individual sites or using a general search engine such as Google is to use the free, full-text, online law journal search engine provided by the Law Practice Division of the American Bar Association.[5] This search engine, which is powered by Google, allows you to perform a free search on the full text of over 400 online law reviews and law journals. Law journals covered by this search engine include many published by Ivy League law schools as well as the *Vanderbilt Law Review, Transactions: The Tennessee Journal of Business Law*, and other law reviews and journals from Tennessee law schools.

Another way to locate online academic law articles is to use the Social Sciences Research Network ("SSRN").[6] SSRN is used by many law professors and some lawyers, judges, and law students to publish free versions of their articles. Often the version published on SSRN may be a draft, a working paper, or in some other way different from the version published in a print journal. However, many authors actually post their work to SSRN before it is published in a journal—often even before it is submitted to journals for publication. This

---

5. The address is http://www.americanbar.org/groups/departments_offices/legal_technology_resources/resources/free_journal_search.html.
6. The address is http://www.ssrn.com.

means that SSRN can be the best source, in some instances, for the most recent work and commentary on cutting-edge legal issues. While some SSRN features are available only to subscribers, the vast majority of papers posted there can be downloaded for free.

2. Indexes

Indexes to law review articles can be an extremely valuable tool in locating relevant materials. Because databases of law review articles tend to be huge, entering search terms that search only the text of the entire article can bring back results that are in the hundreds, if not thousands, of articles, with many of them being completely irrelevant to your issue. If you search an index, your search terms will be matched against words used in the title of the article, in the abstract (brief summary), and against key words chosen by human editors as most closely describing the subject of the article. You can also search for articles by a particular author or published in a specific journal. Doing these narrowly tailored searches can make your results much more precise and relevant. In addition, indexes tend to have broader coverage of materials than full-text databases. For example, a full-text database may only have articles going back to the year 2000, while an index database could contain references to articles published more than 100 years ago.

The two most common indexes of law journal articles are LegalTrac, which provides indexing from over 850 law journals and legal publications since 1980, and Index to Legal Periodicals (ILP), which indexes articles from legal journals, bar publications, and book reviews.[7] Many law libraries subscribe to either LegalTrac or a version of ILP.

Westlaw and Lexis Advance both currently provide access to the same legal journal index, Legal Resource Index (LRI). LRI covers articles from 1980 forward to the current time. Although LRI does not contain the full text of articles, if Westlaw or Lexis Advance has the full text of a particular article, the index entry in LRI will link to the article within that service, making access seamless. On either service, to access LRI, just enter *Legal Resource Index* into the universal search bar. Currently, Bloomberg Law does not include a legal journal index of articles.

---

7. ILP is available in several varieties. The standard ILP product indexes articles published since 1982. A separate database, ILP Retrospective, covers articles published between 1908 and 1981. ILP: Current & Retrospective, combines these products to index articles published between 1908 and the current time.

3. Full-Text Articles on Westlaw, Lexis Advance, and Bloomberg Law

Westlaw and Lexis Advance provide large databases of full-text legal journal articles. Bloomberg Law provides access to a significantly smaller database of legal journal articles. If you search these databases, remember that, although they are large, they are not comprehensive. For example, on Westlaw, full coverage of the *Tennessee Law Review* starts in 1993.[8] On Lexis Advance, you will not find any articles from the *Florida Law Review*, the flagship law journal from the University of Florida.

There are differences in searching the indexes and the full-text databases. Each index record includes bibliographic information such as the title, author, date of publication, and abstract. But the index editors add subject headings — standardized language that may not appear in the title (or text) — that might better match your search terms. In contrast, when you search the full-text databases, you can search every word in every article in each database but there are no subject headings or standardized language added. Full-text searching may allow you to retrieve additional relevant articles that you might miss if you only search index databases. Retrieving additional articles can be a double-edged, sword, though: consider whether you may call up too many articles to efficiently and effectively review for relevance and quality.

Another search strategy to consider is using the advanced search features available on Westlaw and Lexis Advance. After browsing to the appropriate law review/journal database, click the "Advanced" or "Advanced Search" link near the universal search bar. Using the advanced search features will allow you to search for articles by a particular author, in a specific journal, with certain words or phrases in the title or abstract, and in a given date range. In this way, you can combine some of the advantages of searching index fields with the accessibility of using a full-text database.

Which strategy is best will depend upon your research needs; knowing the differences between these approaches will facilitate a better decision.

4. HeinOnline

HeinOnline, another source for accessing law review articles online, has grown in significance since beginning in 2000. The Hein Publishing Company began scanning full runs of most academic law journals beginning with the first volume of each journal. Within several years, Hein completed this retroac-

---

8. This is not an unusual case. Coverage for most law reviews on both Westlaw and Lexis Advance typically starts in the 1990s.

tive process. In addition to including the searchable full text of all articles from each volume for each journal, Hein allows you to browse the table of contents for each volume. Most importantly, all the pages are available as PDF images, which many researchers find more comfortable to read online and easier to cite correctly. HeinOnline is a subscription product available at law school libraries and increasingly in law firms.[9]

5. Google Scholar

Google Scholar searches many scholarly databases with Google's powerful search engine, including several databases that contain law review articles (such as HeinOnline). Searching is a free service provided by Google, but accessing the articles may require a paid subscription, depending on the database linked by Google. Google Scholar does partner with academic libraries to integrate links to materials purchased by the library. Thus, if you are doing research on your computer via a campus network, Google Scholar will recognize your location and enable free access to any journals that the campus library subscribes to.

6. Other Types of Legal Periodicals

Bar journals, legal newspapers, and legal newsletters are often sources for the most up-to-date information needed by both legal practitioners and academic researchers.

a. Bar Journals

Most state bar organizations publish a monthly bar journal with articles on legal developments in that state. Bar journal articles are typically much shorter than the articles published in law reviews; they have few footnotes and present issues relevant to practicing attorneys. For example, articles might explain new judicial opinions, statutes, or court rules, as well as discuss various aspects of law firm management.

The *Tennessee Bar Journal*, published monthly, is available in print, on the Tennessee Bar Association's website,[10] and from Westlaw and Lexis Advance. *Tennessee Bar Journal* issues dating back to 1996 are available on the Tennessee Bar Association's website in both searchable and PDF form.

---

9. Many law school libraries are now also able to offer their alumni access to law journal articles through HeinOnline. If you are a law school graduate, you may want to contact your law school's library to see if this service is available.

10. The address is http://www.tba.org/journal/archive.

The American Bar Association publishes the *ABA Journal*, which has articles of general interest to all attorneys. The ABA also publishes related journals devoted to specific practice areas and interest groups, such as the *ABA Family Law Quarterly* and the *GP Solo & Small Firm Lawyer*.

b. Legal Newspapers and Newsletters

At the national level, several fee-based legal newspapers with associated websites include a combination of free and fee-based information. Examples include the *National Law Journal*[11] and the *New York Law Journal*.[12] Some of these journals are also available on the major commercial research services. Lexis Advance has the most coverage of the national legal newspapers.

There are also several free legal news websites, such as Law.com[13] and Find-Law Legal News Pulse.[14] *TBAToday*, an electronic newsletter published daily, provides the most recent Tennessee appellate court decisions, legislative updates, Tennessee Supreme Court rules, orders, ethics opinions, Attorney General opinions and news stories of interest to Tennessee attorneys. Prior issues of this newsletter are all available on the TBA website and are searchable.[15]

D. *American Law Reports*

1. ALR Annotations

American Law Reports (ALR) is a serial publication of selected cases with accompanying articles, called *annotations*, focused on a very narrow legal issue. The seventh ALR series is now being published, though annotations from earlier series are still useful research tools. *American Law Reports Federal*, now in its third series, is a separate part of ALR that focuses only on federal law. *ALR International* is another separate series that focuses on issues of worldwide importance, including international law topics. Although it originally began as a case reporter, ALR is no longer used for that purpose, and the current series no longer publishes cases at all. The value of ALR lies in the annotations, essays that are lengthy but narrow in scope, tending to address legal issues of some controversy or issues of law that are interpreted differently across the United States.

---

11. The address is http://www.nationallawjournal.com.
12. The address is http://www.newyork lawjournal.com.
13. The address is http://www.law.com.
14. The address is http://legalnews.findlaw.com.
15. The address is http://www.tba.org/op_flash.php.

All annotations, called "articles" in the current series, include a detailed table of contents in outline format, references to related secondary authorities, a topical index, and a jurisdictional table of cited authorities. Because the annotations tend to be long, these tools can assist you in locating the portions of the work that address the specific sub-issue you are interested in or that are from your particular jurisdiction. In addition to describing the law, the annotations also provide links to other recommended secondary sources, such as legal encyclopedias and law journal articles. Because of these references, many researchers find the annotations more useful at the beginning of their research process.

Since ALR makes no effort to cover all of American law comprehensively like a legal encyclopedia does, there may not be an annotation directly on point for every legal topic. If an ALR annotation exists for your topic, however, it can be a gold mine of relevant information.

Moreover, ALR annotations are the only source that can provide a list of cases on a specific set of facts with a particular outcome (i.e., which party won). For example, assume you are working on an age discrimination case that turns on the issue of constructive discharge. An ALR annotation can provide a list of cases in which particular facts were held to be a constructive discharge and cases whose facts were held not to be a constructive discharge.[16]

Analyzing the cases in an ALR annotation can help you understand how a particular rule has been applied in your jurisdiction. The annotations usually describe the various interpretations of a point of law throughout the United States, with the different states grouped together by the similar way they've interpreted the relevant law. However, you can use the Table of Cases towards the beginning of the annotation to find cases from the particular jurisdiction that you are researching. In this way, ALR can become a state-specific tool.

2. How to Research an Issue in ALR

The process of researching in ALR involves using relevant search terms to examine an index or search the online text and locate annotations addressing a legal issue. When searching print, use the multi-volume index. Annotations from *ALR Federal* are also included in the multi-volume index. For less sophisticated or less obscure issues, you might try the one-volume, paperback ALR Quick Index.

---

16. *Circumstances Which Warrant Finding of Constructive Discharge in Cases under Age Discrimination in Employment Act (29 U.S.C.A. §621 et seq.)*, 93 A.L.R. Fed. 10 (1989).

Westlaw and Lexis Advance both have current, comprehensive national ALR databases.[17] The databases are updated weekly with new case annotations. The databases include the multi-volume index as well as newly prepared annotations that are not yet released for print publication. Bloomberg Law does not provide access to ALR.

E. Restatements and Principles — American Law Institute

Restatements of the Law are summaries of traditionally common law areas such as contracts, torts, and property. Restatements were initiated because no unifying, broadly applicable statements of law for these subjects existed. Many cases had to be read together in a time-consuming manner to understand the applicable law. Principles of the Law, introduced in the 1990s, are summaries of areas of law as the drafters would like the law to be. Restatements and Principles are produced by the American Law Institute.

1. The Creation of Restatements[18]

Each Restatement summarizes and explains a specific area of the common law, such as contracts and torts. Examples of Restatements include *Restatement of the Law of Contracts* and *Restatement of the Law of Torts*. Restatements are produced by committees composed of academics, practitioners, and judges organized by the American Law Institute (ALI). These committees draft explanations of the common law in rule format — with outline headings similar to statutes, rather than in the narrative format of judicial decisions. The committees, each led by a person called the *reporter*, circulate the drafts among members for review and revision. Each Restatement published by the ALI includes the text of the rules that explain and summarize the common law; commentary on the rules; illustrations; and notes from the reporter. The painstaking process of creating the drafts leading up to a Restatement and the respect earned by the reporter and members of the committee contribute to the high regard in which Restatements are held.

Among secondary sources, Restatements are the most authoritative. A portion of a Restatement can be primary authority only if it is adopted by a court in a particular case. Once a court has adopted a portion of a Restatement, per-

---

17. On Westlaw, the ALR International database is accessed separately. ALR on Lexis Advance does not include ALR International.

18. The process of creation of Principles of the Law is substantially similar to that of Restatements.

suasive secondary authorities include the committee's commentary and illustrations, notes provided by the reporter, and cases from other jurisdictions that have adopted the Restatement.

2. Researching an Issue in the Restatements or Principles

To begin researching using print Restatements or Principles, locate the applicable Restatement or Principles, which will typically be a multi-volume set. Find the index in the last volume before the appendix. Although the text of the Restatement or Principles itself may only be updated every few decades, the cases that cite to it are updated at least once a year and summarized in pocket parts in the back of the books.

Although the Restatements and Principles are not available freely on the Internet, they may be found online on Westlaw, Lexis Advance, and HeinOnline. For example, on Westlaw, begin typing *restatement* in the universal search bar and a list of the Restatement-related databases will appear. On HeinOnline, go to the American Law Institute Library to locate individual Restatements and Principles, as well as drafts and early versions of the works. Bloomberg Law does not currently provide access to the Restatements or Principles.

To confirm the latest publications in each series, see the American Law Institute website,[19] which includes a frequently updated publications list. The website also has information about new subjects being added to the latest series of subjects and the various drafts of those new subjects that might be available. Because the texts of the Restatements and Principles are so slowly updated, they are not the best source of information for new or cutting-edge legal issues. Their value lies in the certainty of the basic information comprising the topics they cover.

III. Practitioner-Oriented Secondary Authorities

A. Continuing Legal Education Publications

Many states, including Tennessee, require that each attorney licensed to practice within that state participate in a certain number of hours of legal education classes each year. The topics of these classes range widely, from writing better briefs to the latest updates in eminent domain law in Tennessee. These classes are usually referred to as continuing legal education (CLE). While some CLE classes are aimed at new lawyers just learning the building blocks

---

19. The address is http://www.ali.org.

of practice, many CLE courses are intended to offer insights on innovative legal issues.

Presenters at these classes usually prepare handouts that include summaries and details of the topics covered as well as sample forms and checklists. CLE materials are typically very practical in nature. They discuss either how the law has recently changed or how a legal process or procedure might be better accomplished or improved. The materials have current awareness value and may also be useful for a researcher not familiar with the issues related to a legal subject. These handouts may be published by the company or organization sponsoring the CLE class. While CLE materials can provide much valuable information, and can be particularly helpful when researching the law specific to Tennessee, they do have drawbacks. They usually do not have indices, and since they are not supplemented, they tend to go out of date quickly.

The largest publisher of Tennessee CLE materials is the National Business Institute (NBI). Many of NBI's more popular courses are repeated each year, meaning that a new volume of materials on the same topic is published annually. NBI's course materials can be purchased in print or in a PDF format. The courses themselves can be streamed on demand.[20] When researching using CLE materials, make sure that you have the most recently published volume on your topic. Several companies coordinate CLE events at the national level and publish course handbooks. One way to locate CLE materials is to search the library catalog by author, using the name of a CLE publisher as the author. For example, the Practising Law Institute (PLI) sells hundreds of publications from CLE programs via its website[21] and on-demand webcasts are also available. Bloomberg Law provides many of the PLI publications or other CLE-type materials accessible in various databases. Westlaw and Lexis Advance provide other types of CLE materials. Unfortunately, Tennessee-based CLE materials are not regularly made accessible on any of the large online legal research services. As with many secondary sources, CLE materials are typically not freely available on the Internet.

B. Legal Forms

Legal work must be done in a precise manner. Legal processes that have proved successful over time or been tested in the courtroom are replicated as forms that are acceptable or safe methods of accomplishing certain legal tasks. Forms might be used extensively in some aspects of law practice, such as certain

---

20. NBI's website is http://www.nbi-sems.com/.
21. The address is http://www.pli.edu.

types of judicial pleadings, real estate transactions, and wills and estates. By using forms, lawyers or researchers do not have to reinvent the wheel and can be comfortable knowing that a particular form has been successful in the past.

The first challenge of using forms is to know that you have selected the most applicable form. There are many publications that either include forms or are composed entirely of forms. Some of these form sets also include citations to primary law as authority for use of each particular form. A number of form books are available in academic law libraries. Some forms are also available online, providing the ability to complete the forms online or cut and paste at least portions of them into word processing software.

Take care in using any form. Forms are designed for general circumstances, not for your particular client's situation. Before using a form, make sure that you understand every word in the form and modify the form to suit your client's needs. Do not simply fill in the blanks and assume that the form correctly represents your client's position. Unless a particular form is prescribed or approved by a statute or by the court,[22] revise the wording to eliminate unnecessary "legalese" — standard legal jargon that has traditionally been added to legal documents, making them harder to understand than may be necessary.

Most jurisdictions have forms that are specific to the laws and methods of that jurisdiction. While some state-specific collections of forms may not contain the volume or depth of various types of forms found in one of the national form books, the forms available in a state-specific set are more relevant to the unique aspects of that jurisdiction. Tennessee has several general-purpose form sets, such as *Gore's Forms for Tennessee Annotated*; Robinson's *Tennessee Forms*; and Leveille's two sets, *Tennessee Legal and Business Forms* and *Litigation Forms and Analysis*. Other form books may be directed toward a specific area of law and are more likely to be national in scope rather than focused on one state such as Tennessee. *Fletcher Corporate Forms Annotated* is one of many sets of business forms intended for a national audience.

West's Legal Forms and *American Jurisprudence Legal Forms, 2d* are examples of national form book sets. Although not focused on a particular jurisdiction, these form books are very detailed and provide a form that could be adapted to nearly any situation; however, you carry the burden of knowing and understanding exactly what is required in your jurisdiction and meeting your client's needs. These publications and other national form books are available online either from Westlaw or Lexis Advance, depending on the publisher.

---

22. For example, Tennessee Rule of Appellate Procedure 48 approves the use of the forms set out in an appendix to the Rules.

Westlaw, Lexis Advance, and Bloomberg Law all have large collections of forms and sample documents online. These forms are searchable and browsable by topic and jurisdiction. Bloomberg's Dealmaker database is a collection of the best sample documents selected by Bloomberg staff.

A number of companies provide legal forms via the Internet, such as U.S. Legal Forms[23] and FindLaw Forms.[24] Forms of this nature typically are not free but are provided for a small fee, usually less than the cost of having the correct form or document prepared by a licensed attorney. These forms tend to be general in nature but might profess to be appropriate for various jurisdictions.

In addition, briefs and memoranda can also serve as forms. Some law firms and advocacy organizations maintain brief banks allowing staff or associated members to access the group's previous work on a similar topic. These documents can be used as a starting point for further drafting and research, with appropriate updating and modifications. Briefs, memoranda, and other court filings may also be accessed on Westlaw, Lexis Advance, and Bloomberg Law, though pricing may make them quite expensive outside of the academic realm.

C. Jury Instructions

Most jurisdictions have prepared standard jury instructions, often called pattern jury instructions, to be used by the judge to instruct the jury in various areas of law relevant to an issue in the trial. The drafters of pattern jury instructions attempt to provide succinct statements of all of the elements of a cause of action, or of the basis for damages or a particular defense. Thus, pattern jury instructions are quite useful to lawyers who are marshaling their facts and arguments in preparation for trial.

They can also be enormously helpful to a beginning researcher seeking to understand the basic elements of a given claim or defense in her jurisdiction. Pattern jury instructions typically include references to the primary authorities from which they were derived, for example, the pertinent parts of the *Tennessee Code Annotated* and important case opinions that set out the elements of a particular cause of action or defense.

The Tennessee Judicial Conference has committees on pattern jury instructions for both criminal and civil matters. Their publications, *Tennessee Pattern Jury Instructions — Criminal* and *Tennessee Pattern Jury Instructions — Civil*,

---

23. The address is http://www.uslegalforms.com.
24. The address is http://forms.lp.findlaw.com.

ᴈd in volumes 7 and 8, respectively, of the set *Tennessee Practice.*
ᴑ available online on Westlaw, Lexis Advance, and Bloomberg Law.
ιre referenced by Tennessee lawyers and judges by their initials:
T.P.I.—Civil and T.P.I—Criminal. The pattern jury instructions are not
mandatory. As the preface to the civil set notes, "they are offered merely as a
guide, not a straitjacket."

Many of the federal circuits also prepare and publish pattern jury instructions
for use in that circuit. Some circuits publish only criminal or civil jury instructions, while others publish both. The Sixth Circuit, to which Tennessee belongs,
has published its own *Pattern Criminal Jury Instructions* for use in criminal
trials.[25] Most federal pattern jury instructions are freely accessible on the appropriate federal circuit court webpage.[26] Many may also be available in print
in your law library.

Lexis publishes *Modern Federal Jury Instructions*, a five-volume set encompassing many areas of both civil and criminal law that are frequently litigated
in federal courts. While these model instructions are drafted by editorial staff
at LexisNexis, they draw, in some parts, from the official instructions published
by various federal appellate courts. This set is also available on Lexis Advance.
Model jury instructions are also available for specific areas of law, such as an-
titrust and patent litigation. These may be drafted by the staff of a commercial
publisher, or, more typically, by a national organization such as the American
Bar Association. Again, these types of model jury instructions may be useful
to a legal researcher looking for a succinct introduction to an area of law.

D. Uniform Laws and Model Codes

Uniform laws and model codes are written by organizations that hope to
harmonize the statutory laws of the fifty states. The most active of these organizations is the National Conference of Commissioners on Uniform State
Laws, now known as the Uniform Law Commission. Each state is responsible
for selecting the judges, jurists, professors, and legislators to be members of
the Commission. The commissioners attend the national meetings of the Commission to work on preparing and adopting the uniform laws and codes.

---

25. The Sixth Circuit's Criminal Pattern Jury Instructions can be found at http://
www.ca6.uscourts.gov/internet/crim_jury_insts.htm.
26. *Federal Evidence Review* provides a handy compilation of online pattern jury
instructions, including federal, by subject, and selected state jury instructions. This
resource can be found at http://federalevidence.com/evidence-resources/federal-jury-
instructions. However, use caution: this site is not always as up-to-date as it might be.

The most widely available print publication of the Commission's work is a West publication called *Uniform Laws Annotated*, which is also available on Westlaw. The print version is updated at least annually.

The most important example of the Commission's work is the Uniform Commercial Code (UCC), which has been widely adopted by states across the country. In addition to the proposed statutory language of each code, the Commission also publishes explanatory notes, drafts, and comments about the proposed code.

Uniform laws and model codes are not particularly persuasive unless one or more of its provisions has been adopted in your jurisdiction. When a uniform law or model code is adopted, its explanatory notes become highly persuasive secondary authority. Judicial opinions from other states that adopted the same code provisions would also be highly persuasive when interpreting your state's statute.

E. Law-Related Blogs

A wide variety of legal commentary is available in blogs. Law-related blogs, sometimes called "blawgs," are usually as valuable as the reputations of the authors. Blog commentary from a recognized expert in a legal area could assist a research project in the same way that commentary from a treatise might. Even commentary from less well known blog authors could provide useful information when researching a topic. But because blogs are often not edited, you must filter through a great deal of commentary and make your own assessment of the value and quality of the information. This is a common problem when using free Internet resources. Additionally, one of the dangers in searching law-related blogs for legal research purposes, besides the challenge of determining the value and quality of the information, is the possibility of using too much time to find information of little relevance.

Potential blog authors or topics can be identified using a search engine such as Google; however, perhaps the best approach to finding quality law-related blogs is to use the Blawg Directory at the American Bar Association Journal website.[27] Currently, the directory is browsable by topic, author type, region, law school, and court. The directory is continuously updated. The Tennessee Bar Association provides an online directory of blogs of interest to the Tennessee legal community as well.[28]

---

27. The address is http://www.abajournal.com/blawgs.
28. The address is http:// www.tba.org/law-related-blog-directory.

IV. Selecting the Most Appropriate Secondary Authority

Secondary authorities have different strengths and weaknesses and can be used in different ways while researching. Which authority you use will depend on your research project and what is available to you. For a broad overview of an area of law, an encyclopedia may be best. For an in-depth scholarly analysis on a narrower topic, a law review article is more likely to be helpful. On cutting-edge issues, blogs, CLE materials, and bar journals may be useful, as these sources often cover new areas of law promptly. In litigation, forms and pattern jury instructions may prove indispensable.

If you understand those strengths and weaknesses, you will be able to select the most useful type of secondary authority for your research project. Researchers are typically working under time constraints and do not have time to review an extensive array of secondary materials. Rather, twenty or thirty minutes spent browsing a few carefully selected authorities can pay dividends in time and understanding. See Table 7-1 for an outline of selecting appropriate secondary authorities for a research project. Table 7-2 summarizes the strengths and weaknesses of the five traditional secondary authorities.

Table 7-1. Outline for Selecting Appropriate Secondary Authorities for a Research Project

1. Determine what you are trying to accomplish with your research. Are you searching for a quick, broad overview of a legal topic or a deep but narrowly focused description of a discrete area of law? Do you need criticism and analysis of existing law? Do you need recommendations for changes in the law?

2. Examine the chart in **Table 7-2** explaining the strengths and weaknesses of the five traditional secondary sources.

3. Match the purpose of your research with one or two secondary sources having strengths in areas addressing your research goal. For example, a legal encyclopedia will provide a broad, descriptive overview of a legal topic. An *American Law Reports* annotation will drill down deep into a narrow topic, providing description and citations to primary law in multiple jurisdictions, but will provide no criticism or analysis.

Table 7-2. Secondary Authority Characteristics

	Organization	Currency	Depth	Descriptive or Analytical	Reputation	Updating
Restatements	Published separately by broad topic, such as contracts or torts.	Varies but tends to be among the least current of secondary authorities.	Great depth, with many examples and much commentary.	Describes what the law is, with examples and notes.	Highest. Frequently cited by courts and leading scholars.	Case citations are updated frequently, but the text itself is updated rarely.
Treatises	Published separately by topic. Available for nearly every legal topic.	Varies. Be sure to check publication and supplement dates. Not as current as journal articles or ALR.	Broad, well-organized coverage, typically with great depth.	Typically both describes the law and offers commentary and critique.	High, depending on the individual author.	May be updated annually or less frequently.
Periodicals (Law reviews and journals)	Not organized by topic. Each issue of a law review usually has articles on many unrelated topics.	Most current, along with ALRs.	Usually very deep focus on a narrow issue or sub-issue.	Often provides both description of the law and analysis and critique.	Varies depending on reputation of author and journal.	Not updated per se. If article is out of date, search for more recent article on same issue.
ALR Annotations	Not organized by topic. Locate relevant annotations by searching or using index.	Most current, along with periodicals.	Very deep focus on a narrow issue.	Description of the law and comparison of the law in different jurisdictions, but no commentary or analysis.	Slightly better than encyclopedias.	New annotations are constantly published. New case citations are added regularly to existing annotations.
Encyclopedias	Organized by topic, with topics arranged alphabetically within set.	Poor. Very slow to add new legal topics and theories.	Covers a broad range of topics, but not with much depth.	Description only.	Low persuasiveness in most instances.	Annual pocket parts that consist mostly of updated case citations.

Chapter 8

Research Strategies and Organization

I. Planning Your Research Strategy[1]

A. Initial Inquiries

Before beginning the research process, you must gather facts from the client or the person for whom you are researching. In the typical practice of law, gathering facts involves interviewing a client and perhaps witnesses; reviewing relevant documents; and speaking with colleagues or other professionals with relevant information or experience.

Another initial inquiry is determining which jurisdiction's law applies to the issue. Is it a federal law issue or a state law issue? If the issue will be addressed by state law, which state? Where did the action occur? Who are the actors and where do they live? If both federal and state law may be applicable, how will they interact? The rules of civil or criminal procedure, and possibly other law, will determine the answers to these questions. The good news is that the basic research process outlined in this book is applicable in every jurisdiction. Note that you may need to research the jurisdictional issue before beginning to research the legal issue itself. Gathering the facts and addressing some of these questions will enable you to write an issue statement, a description of what you are researching.

B. Varying the Research Process

The research process presented in Chapter 1 contains seven steps: (1) generate a list of *research terms*; (2) consult *secondary authorities*; (3) find controlling *constitutional provisions*, *statutes*, *regulations*, or *rules*; (4) find citations to relevant *case law*; (5) read the full text of the cases; (6) *update* your primary

---

1. This portion of the chapter is drawn from *Oregon Legal Research* and is used with permission.

authorities using a citator such as KeyCite, Shepard's, or BCite; and (7) determine that you are finished when you *encounter the same authorities* and no new authorities through all the research methods you employ. When you are conducting research in an unfamiliar area of law, you should begin with secondary authorities and work through the process step by step.

After learning how to use each of the resources listed in the seven research steps, you can modify this basic process and design a research strategy that is appropriate for a specific project. For example, if you are familiar with a relevant statute, your research may be more effective if you go directly to an annotated code. As another example, if a supervisor gives you a citation to a case she knows is relevant, you may want to begin by updating the case or using its topics and key numbers from the headnotes on Westlaw or in a West digest. Finally, if your supervisor knows that the issue is controlled by common law, you may feel comfortable not researching statutory or constitutional provisions, or spending very little time in those areas.

Even for novices, and especially for experienced researchers, the research process is not necessarily linear. You will use research terms in searching the indexes of secondary authorities and statutes as well as cases; in other words, you will use information from Step 1 in Step 2 and Step 4. Secondary authorities may cite relevant statutes or cases, taking you from Step 2 to either Step 3 or Step 4. Updating in Step 6 may reveal more cases that you need to read or it may uncover a new law review article that is on point, meaning you would return to Step 5 or Step 2.

As you learn more about a project, you may want to review whether your earlier research was effective. Even as you begin writing, you may need to do more research if new issues arise or if you need more support for an argument. Accordingly, keeping a good record of the sources you have consulted and authorities you have read is essential to your efficiency as a researcher and for others who may become involved in the project.

C. Creating Your Research Plan

The first document you should create before you begin substantive research is your *research plan*. Particularly novice legal researchers find that writing up your research plan will help you clarify issues and think about where to begin. A sample research plan can be seen in Table 8-1. You may want to devise a generic research plan of your own and keep it available. Having a research plan as a form with questions already included is much more organized and efficient than simply writing down lists of words or sources. If you were using the form

Table 8-1. Sample Research Plan

Issue Statement	*Is a county library system, which is a unit of county government, an "entity of the state"?*
Jurisdiction	*Start with Tennessee, expand to other states if no applicable authority.*
Known relevant authorities	*Tennessee statute passed two years ago requiring government-issued identification in order to vote.*
Terms of art or legal jargon to define before beginning research	*None*
Research terms	*County, county government, unit of county government, state, entity of the state, identification, voter identification, election, library*
Possible secondary authorities	*ALR, law review articles, treatise on election law*
Possible statutes	*Tennessee Code Annotated — voter identification statutes and statutes on county government/ government entities*
Possible regulations	*Election regulations, if any*
Case law databases or reporters	*Tennessee case law databases, West's South Western Reporter*
Period of time to research	*Current*
Follow-up questions for supervising attorney	*Has anyone else in the office worked on this issue recently?*
Due date and desired format of work product	*Office memorandum due Monday, July 3*

in Table 8-1, you would keep the right-hand column blank on your master copy and fill in the blanks for each new research project you were assigned.

Imagine that you are just starting your first legal clerking job at a public interest law firm in Nashville. You are called into the assigning attorney's office and told the following:

Two years ago, the Tennessee General Assembly passed a law requiring voters to present identification "issued by an entity of the state government." The Knox County Public Library has begun issuing photo identification on request to anyone who holds a Knox County Public Library card. In the recent presidential primary election, five Knox County residents attempted to vote and presented the library identification cards as required government-issued identification. Election officials refused to accept the identification, although they did allow the voters to vote with provisional ballots, which have not been counted. We will be representing these voters and filing a lawsuit seeking an injunction ordering election officials to count the ballots. Although there are many issues implicated in this lawsuit, confine your research to whether a county government and/or unit of the county government is an "entity of the state." Please give me a memorandum on this issue next Monday.

Having a research plan form that you regularly use will make a new project seem less overwhelming, since the plan will set out boundaries for your research and suggest the steps you need to take for each project. Furthermore, if you keep the habit of working with your form and taking it with you to meetings with supervisors, you will have a better chance of getting all the information you need to begin researching right away. This means you won't have to repeatedly go back to your supervisor to clarify issues such as jurisdiction or due date that the attorney neglected to mention and you forgot to ask about in your meeting.

You should refer to the research plan frequently to be sure you are on track. Feel free to revise your strategy as you learn more about the issues. For instance, you may read a case with a related cause of action that you had not considered or you may encounter an article that highlights a new angle that you had not known of earlier. If so, you need to adjust your research accordingly. If you are working with other attorneys on the project, however, be sure to consult with them before delving into research of additional issues, to avoid duplication of effort.

When you are developing your research plan, the issue statement and research terms are the most crucial parts for conducting effective legal research. Be willing to spend some time on your issue statement to ensure it is precise. Then try to develop an expansive list of research terms, and refer to this list as you begin work in each new source. Note on the list which terms were helpful in which resource. Add new terms to the list as you discover them. This list is especially likely to grow during your initial efforts if you begin with a secondary source that provides context for the research project.

D. Choosing Between Print and Various Online Sources of Legal Information[2]

A fluent, effective legal researcher will be able to confidently research using any combination of various commercial databases, free Internet sources, and print materials, and will be able to adapt quickly to new situations and new requirements. Generally, understanding how print sources are organized and

---

2. This portion of the chapter is drawn from *North Carolina Legal Research*, and is used with permission.

produced leads to better online research, as many online products are still based conceptually on the print versions of the same materials.

In the modern research environment, you often have a choice of where and how to access the information you need when deciding where to search for relevant law or legal commentary to address the issue being researched. Access to digital information from online vendors such as West (Thomson Reuters), LexisNexis, and Bloomberg are often the format of choice for a growing number of purposes. Lower-cost online vendors such as Fastcase and Casemaker also provide access to smaller but substantial amounts of legal information. Additionally, the federal government and many state governments are now posting legal information on free government websites. Governments are beginning to develop ways of authenticating the digital information on their web pages, making them more reliable. Finally, traditional print publications are still available to some researchers and may be the most efficient or affordable alternative source.

Confronted with an amazing array of sources of legal information that is growing every day, a savvy researcher gives careful consideration to the choice of format for legal information. The following seven considerations are some of the more important factors involved in making that decision: availability, cost, accuracy, age, context, efficiencies, and confidentiality. Each raises important questions for the researcher to answer. The seven considerations are intertwined with each other, and it's difficult to consider any one without involving one of the others.

1. Availability

While most traditional legal print sources of primary law are still being published, increasingly law libraries in law firms and law schools alike are not purchasing this format due to cost or space issues. It is likely that some traditional print legal publications will cease being published in the near future as their costs rise and customers choose not to purchase them. The most recent primary law is available online either from fee-based vendors or a free government website. While the editorial enhancements may vary widely from one online source to another, the text of the law should be consistent in all of these reputable sources. You will be better able to judge after reading this book the value of the editorial enhancements that are only available at a premium, from a few online sources.

Unlike primary law, authoritative secondary sources and other valuable commentary are less likely to be available for free online. When respected secondary authorities are available online, they are often very expensive. The number of less authoritative legal commentaries on the Internet is growing. The price is right, but are they accurate and currently updated, and by whom?

2. Cost

The cost of a print publication is a one-time charge for ownership of the information, although the publication may require updating weekly, quarterly, or annually at a substantial cost, and the cost of purchasing and storing print resources continues to rise. The benefit is that the purchaser may use the publication as often as desired without additional cost. How might the indirect cost of using this information be recaptured from the client?

Alternatively, online information may be priced in various ways. One pricing model is a flat rate contract for unlimited access to databases over a specific period of time. Or, an online service might have a per-use access fee so that the researcher is charged each time she accesses the database, which is more easily itemized for clients. If your office does not have a flat-rate access package with a particular online provider, the costs of searching can be tremendous. Factors that affect those costs can include the number of minutes you are logged on, the number of searches you conduct, the size of the databases you search, and how many documents you choose to view, download, or print. A single research project, poorly conceived and sloppily done, could costs hundreds or thousands of dollars.[3] Be sure you know the billing practices of your office before deciding to use online sources that are not free: What is your office's contract with the online provider? How will your office pass along charges to clients? How much are the clients willing to pay? Are there any databases that are considered off-limits to the attorneys, due to the expense? When you do pro bono work, will the office cover the costs of online searches?

Other online pricing structures are possible, and much information is available for free. Many government organizations are posting law on government websites that are freely available. But if these sites are poorly organized, what is the cost of the additional time lost searching for the free information? If the information is not as currently updated as information from premium services, what is the cost of the additional time and effort required for more extensive

---

3. Even if your office does have a flat-rate access package, keep in mind that extensive use of paid databases in the current year by people in your firm will often mean that the price of the package next year will be much higher. Therefore, it is always prudent to try to be as efficient as possible on Lexis, Westlaw, and Bloomberg, even if your office subscribes to a flat rate unlimited use access plan.

updating? Also, what is the cost in time and efficiency when using free databases of not having the editorial enhancements found in premium databases?

The role that cost plays in selecting the best format is complicated and very individualized. What is the value of your client's case or your research project? Do you have a client who is willing to pay a premium for costs incurred in researching the relevant law? In law practice, consider whether the financial value returned from your research offsets the expense invested in using high cost resources. If not, are there less expensive alternative sources of information that would lower the costs? Additional considerations involving cost might include what information your firm or organization has already purchased or what online licenses the firm has already entered into for access to legal information.

3. Accuracy

Researchers of all types expect the information that they find to be accurate. Print material generally tends to be more accurate than online material simply because of the enhanced editorial process and the resulting high level of reliability found in print publications. Depending upon the source, websites sometimes lack professional editing and certainly many sites contain information that has not been as thoroughly edited as the process for editing books. For a book to appear in a law library, the publisher must first have decided the material in the book had some value. The publisher and author would likely have edited the document numerous times. Next, a law librarian must have decided that the book would enhance the collection. The publisher, author, and librarian would need to make careful decisions to protect their reputations. Because of this careful process, print material tends to be more accurate than online versions of the same documents. Now, of course, the value of an edited book may be available as an ebook, accessible through a law library or a vendor, perhaps providing the best of both worlds for some purposes.

In contrast to the time-intensive, formal publishing process, many online materials are often made available very quickly, making those materials valuable to researchers for whom current awareness is critical. This rapid availability means, though, that even reputable services may post documents with a less thorough editing process. Trusted sources like Westlaw, Lexis Advance, and Bloomberg Law tend to have more typographical errors in their online documents than in their print counterparts. Government websites are usually highly reliable, but even the online documents that governments post may not be considered "official." For example, the official version of a Tennessee judicial decision is found in *West's South Western Reporter*; the version posted by the

Tennessee Supreme Court on its own website is unofficial.[4] There is a nationwide movement to develop more reliability in government digital information that will slowly address this problem.[5]

Accuracy is a particular concern if the information provider is not an organization that traditionally edits information. Be extremely leery of documents that you find hosted on websites that allow anyone to post anything on a personal website. Look at the domain name of the website: government sites ending in *.gov, *.mil, or *.us; educational sites ending in *.edu; or non-profit organization sites ending in *.org are generally considered to provide higher-quality information than what you can find posted on someone's personal website.

High-quality sites containing reliable information will usually identify when they were last updated. Depending on the type of materials presented, that date will generally be quite recent. Good, reliable sites will include links to help navigate or search the site. They will often provide contact information for the person or organization responsible for the site, and that contact information will be more than just an email address.

You may also wish to check to see whether the site you are looking at is well thought of by others. You can use Google by typing in *link:* followed immediately (no space) by the URL of the site you are researching. This search will generate a list of sites that link to the site you are researching. If your site is linked to by many other reputable organizations' websites, that would be a reliable indicator of high quality.

This is a period of transition concerning the accepted reliability of many digital sources, especially open source sites such as Wikipedia. Sources such as Wikipedia are now widely used by many legal researchers including judges.[6] Casetext.com is a newer example of a constantly evolving site that is growing through free contributions from various people.[7] The best practice for now is

---

4. More and more, however, state governments are designating online versions of their authorities as official versions. For example, Tennessee's administrative code and register are both available only online, and the state's electronic version is considered official.

5. See the *Uniform Electronic Legal Material Act*, already adopted in some states, but not yet in Tennessee. http://www.uniformlaws.org/Act.aspx?title=Electronic+Legal+Material+Act

6. *See* Debra Cassens Weiss, "The Supreme Court Spurns Wikipedia, But Federal Appeals Courts Cited It Nearly 100 Times in Five Years," ABA Journal (Apr. 24, 2012) http://www.abajournal.com/news/article/the_supreme_court_spurns_wikipedia_but_federal_appeals_courts_cited_it_near .

7. The address is https://casetext.com.

to always verify information from an unknown or less reputable source, including Wikipedia. The use of online information requires a higher level of evaluation of the accuracy of the information.

4. Age

Because law is constantly changing and evolving, the publication date of information can be critically important for researchers. Printed information is usually marked with a publication or copyright date. Printed supplements to books meant to update the contents are also typically dated. Online databases are usually, but not always, more current than print publications. Many researchers incorrectly assume a database is currently updated, simply because it is online. You should always find the publication date for any information relied upon in the research process.

You should also question the period of time covered by an online database. Online information vendors often provide a "scope note" explaining how often a database is updated or perhaps providing the date it was last updated. Be sure to check every online site or database you use for its scope of coverage, if that information is available. For instance, some online sites may contain materials from only the last few years. If you are researching tort law, and the leading res ipsa loquitur case from your jurisdiction was published sixty years ago, you might have a very hard time locating it online using only free websites. Finding older material may require either using print sources or a premium online source in some instances.

5. Context

The ability to see the broader picture is usually an important element of effective legal research. Information read out of context might be misinterpreted or misunderstood. The ability to browse a table of contents and to view related text surrounding relevant information is critical. The need for context is particularly strong when researching statutory or regulatory information, or commentary such as that found in legal treatises or encyclopedias. The traditional nature and structure of print publications facilitates this element.

Fortunately, an increasing number of online sources include tables of contents, hyperlinked outlines, browsable page formats, and indexes. Online database services, such as Westlaw, Lexis Advance, and Bloomberg Law, as well as state and federal government providers, are increasingly including top-level browsability as a display option. These tools can provide context so that you can understand the big picture before concentrating on a narrow legal issue. They can also help you make sure that you have found all relevant materials, rather than just the few portions of an online text that exactly correspond to the precise words you used in your search query. When searching online, use these tools whenever they are available. Clicking on a table of contents link can show you where your document is placed within related material. This tactic is especially helpful when an online search takes you to the middle of a document and you need context to understand how that document relates to the bigger picture.

6. Efficiencies

Efficiencies are typically very individualized to a specific researcher. For example, some researchers are more comfortable than others reading pages of text online. More objectively, however, print generally provides superior context, which might be more important early in the research process where the researcher's work is less focused and the researcher benefits from exposure to a wide array of information.

Online research has a number of advantages. Online research is more efficient when searching for a known document using specific information. Consider also the additional online efficiencies concerning the convenience of accessing information and either printing or downloading relevant documents. Most significant among those are ease of searching, the ability to navigate among hyperlinked documents, the convenience of downloading or printing important documents, and the frequency with which many online sources are updated.

a. How much do you know about the topic?

When a field of law or particular issue is new to you, you may have difficulty identifying the right search terms to generate relevant results with online keyword searching. You may not know the terms of art used by lawyers, legislators, or judges when discussing your issue, or you may not realize that a particular defense, cause of action, or theory is likely to figure prominently into case opinions about your topic. If this is a new field of law or issue for you, it is probably safest and most efficient to start in a secondary authority (online or in print) where you can scan a table of contents and browse through relevant portions of the book. Once you feel comfortable with an area of law, you can move on to do efficient online searching.

b. Are your search terms likely to be broad or narrow?

List your likely search terms. How general or specific are they? Are they likely to be used in many different contexts, only some of which would be relevant to your research? If so, it may be best to start researching in browsable materials. For example, if you were researching when police detention of a possible witness or suspect turned into arrest for purposes of Miranda rights, your search terms might include words such as police, detain, detention, arrest, interrogation, warning, and Miranda. All of these terms could be used in myriad legal situations and could very well appear in a tremendously high number of opinions in criminal cases in the country—the vast majority of which would have nothing to do with what you are researching. Trying to find a way to tell the computer exactly what you want in this situation will be difficult. But by browsing a digital or print book on search and seizure law and skimming through the table of contents, you could quickly and easily discover the important issues and leading authorities in that area of law.

If, on the other hand, you can quickly come up with specific search terms, then it may be more efficient to start research using those specific search terms online. For instance, if you are trying to find and summarize cases in which someone was injured because a car's air bag failed to deploy in an accident, you have some very good and specific search terms to work with, such as air bag, airbag, accident, crash, deploy, and inflate. Online keyword searches in case law databases would likely be a strong strategy.

7. Confidentiality

Attorneys are obligated to keep certain information private and may decide to keep other information confidential as a matter of strategy. Not all websites or online services guarantee the level of confidentiality needed in some circumstances. When using an online service, it is important to consider the privacy of your activity. This includes the safety of your device (such as a PC, laptop, or phone), the network (such as your office network or wireless Internet offered at a coffee shop), and the website itself. While the same information may be available on multiple online systems, each website or service may have different policies about what information is tracked, saved, and shared with third parties. Reviewing privacy policies and ensuring encrypted data transmission may be necessary when conducting sensitive legal research online.

E. Additional Considerations in Searching Online

One of the challenges of using online information and following links from one document to another is the problem of losing track of what kind of information you are viewing. Keeping excellent notes about the various documents you view as you jump from one document to another is the best strategy for maintaining an awareness and understanding of the sources of law or background information you view.

Also, try restricting your search to the smallest database or set of databases that will contain the documents you need. If you only need cases from the Sixth Circuit Court of Appeals, you can be more efficient by searching a database containing just those cases. In addition to producing a more focused set of results, smaller databases also tend to be less expensive than their larger counterparts, depending upon your contract with the research service.

II. Conducting Your Research

A. Taking Notes and Keeping Organized[8]

Take careful notes throughout the research process. Taking notes can help you avoid duplicating steps, especially if you have to interrupt your research for a significant length of time. Research notes also provide a basis for organizing and writing your document. None of these notes have to be formal or typed, but they should at least be organized and readable.

The only "right" way to take notes and keep your research organized is the way that best helps you perform effective research, understand the legal issues, and analyze the problem. You could simply write notes on a pad of paper or on your computer or other device in a single document.

As you work with each new resource, make notes that summarize your work in that resource. For online research, indicate the website or service, the specific searches you entered, filters you used, and databases searched.[9] For print research, indicate the volumes you used, the indexes or tables you used, and the terms for which you searched. List both successful and unsuccessful search terms and searches so that you do not inadvertently repeat these same steps later, so that you can revisit a "dead end" that eventually becomes relevant, and so that you can return to a particularly successful search later and run it again to retrieve more current results. Example notes are in Table 8-2. These

---

8. This portion of the chapter is based on *Oregon Legal Research* and is used with permission.

9. Taking notes on your computer will make recording your searches easier, as you can simply cut and paste the text of your searches from the search box and into your notes.

notes will help you stay on track while avoiding duplicating your research at a later date. Notes will also indicate the time period that needs to be updated as you near your project deadline.[10]

Table 8-2. Example Notes for Online Searching

Date of Search: June 19, 2016

Issue: Whether a covenant not to compete is enforceable in Tennessee

Online Service: Westlaw

Database(s) Searched: Tennessee cases

Search Terms: Covenant, contract, competition, noncompetition, restraint of trade, compete, non-compete, employer, employee, employment.

Date Restriction: Last three years

Search: (Covenant contract) /p (noncompet! "restraint of trade" compet!) /p employ!

Results: [Either list your results here or print a cite list to attach to your notes.]

Do not underestimate the learning process that occurs while taking notes. Deciding what is important enough to include in notes and expressing your reasoning in your own words will increase your understanding of the legal issues involved. Highlighting a printed document does not provide this analytical advantage.

However you choose to keep your notes, you will want one central place to organize your most important authorities and documents. For example, some researchers use Zotero or Endnote to organize their research. Other people find that the most effective way to organize their research projects is to have a three-ring binder with tabs. You should organize your research plan, research notes, citation list for all authorities, cases, statutes (and related authorities such as constitutional provisions or court rules), regulations, and secondary authorities. Although this sort of research organization system may seem elaborate, keep in mind that you may be called off a project at any time, and some

---

10. Although Westlaw, Lexis Advance, and Bloomberg Law all save your prior searches and research information, this information is kept only for a relatively brief period of time. Additionally, one of the purposes of notes is to be able to pass them along to another researcher who takes over for you or joins your team, and relying on history that is part of your personal account on one of these commercial services will defeat that purpose. Also, efficient research in the current digital environment often requires the use of different services. Your complete research "path" will likely not be "saved" in any one research service such as Westlaw.

matters stay open for a long time. Someone else may need to take over for you if you are directed to work on more urgent matters. That person will need to know exactly what you have done and what you found. Also, having all of your research steps and results in an organized and easily understandable system will not only impress your superiors and colleagues, it will make your research more efficient and streamlined, thus saving you time and frustration, and saving your client money.

B. Secondary Authorities

Remember that the text and footnotes of secondary authorities are usually excellent places to find citations to relevant primary authorities. Write a brief summary for each secondary authority you consult — even if it is just to record what search terms you used and the fact that you found nothing relevant. For the more fruitful sources, summarize in your own words the relevant analysis in the source. Always include references to specific pages or paragraphs. Try to include a few sentences about how this source relates to your research. Does it explain the background of a statute? Does it trace the development of a line of cases? Does it criticize the law in your jurisdiction? Does it suggest a novel approach to your problem? Additionally, note any references to primary authorities that may be on point. Remember that your goal is to leave an organized set of research notes that will enable someone new to the project to understand precisely what you have done and what you found without having to retrace your steps.

When working with secondary authorities, resist the urge to click "print." The goals of reading secondary authorities are usually to obtain an overview of an area of law and to locate citations to primary authority. These goals can be met by referring to secondary authorities in the library or by skimming them online, without the waste of printing or copying numerous pages of text.

C. List of Authorities

Create a list of primary authorities that will contain the names and citations of all the authorities that you need to read. Devote one portion of the list to primary authorities and another portion to secondary authorities. Throughout your research, as you come across citations to potentially relevant authorities, include them in your list. This will allow you to maintain your train of thought with one resource while ensuring that you keep track of important cites to check later. If your list contains a number of entries, check for duplicates before reading the authorities.

D. Analytical Notes on Primary Authorities

At frequent points, stop and read the primary authority that you are finding. Legal analysis occurs throughout the process of researching a legal issue; reading as you research will ensure that you are finding relevant material.

Quickly read each authority first to decide whether it is relevant. Your goal here is not to understand every nuance of the document, but to make a decision as to whether it is definitely relevant, is definitely not relevant, or needs further consideration. Making this decision can be time consuming, especially for a novice legal researcher.

To determine the relevancy of statutes and rules, focus primarily on operative language that sets out duties or proscribes certain conduct. Move next to examine the parts of the statute that provide definitions. You should also browse through the statutory sections just before and after the most relevant parts to see if they have a bearing on your issue. Sections setting forth the purpose of the statute or that are plainly not applicable to your client's situation should just be briefly skimmed.

To determine the relevancy of cases, begin by reading the synopsis at the beginning of the case. Then skim the headnotes or core concepts to find the portions of the case that appear to be most relevant, and read those parts of the case first. Finally, skim the procedural history, the facts of the case, and analysis of possibly unrelated points of law.

If the source contains relevant material, make notes on your list of authorities. If it is not relevant, mark it off your list but leave it visible so that you won't accidently forget you already read it and waste time reviewing it again.

Once you have selected a number of relevant authorities, choose an organizational scheme for reading them carefully in groups. If there is a constitutional provision, statute, or rule on point, begin by reading it carefully, then move to reading cases that interpret the provision. One approach is to read cases in reverse chronological order, starting with the most recent. This approach lets you see the current state of the law first. You may find that the more recent cases summarize and explain the older cases, which will help you understand them and read them more efficiently. This approach also helps you avoid spending time learning old law that has been revised or superseded.

Reading cases chronologically may be time consuming for causes of action that have existed for many years. Except for historical research, you may want to impose an artificial cut-off of twenty or thirty years in the past so that you put your effort into recent law. Of course, you should always keep an open mind with respect to your cut-off: if you see hints that an older case may be particularly on point, you should read it carefully regardless of when it was decided.

After you have gone over all relevant authorities initially to assess their importance, you will want to read the more pertinent authorities slowly and carefully. Be sure you understand the procedural posture of each case, since this affects the standard of review applied. Also be sure that you understand the facts of cases. Drawing a timeline or chart of the relationships between the parties may be helpful.

When researching several issues or related claims, consider them one at a time. You may have several lists of authorities, one for each claim you are researching. In particularly complex matters, you may want to create a different organizational file for each claim.

1. Notes on Statutes

Because the exact words of statutes are so important, you should print[11] or save the text of these provisions. If a statute is very short and clear, highlighting the pertinent portions may be sufficient for your purposes. If the statute is long, complex, or requires reference to several other statutory provisions, make a succinct outline of the statute. You should stress those parts of the statute that are most pertinent to your client's situation and note in your outline relationships with other code sections. Creating this outline will help you understand the statute and its application to the issue you are researching.

2. Notes on Cases

When you decide that a case is relevant, you should brief it. The brief does not have to follow any formal style. The brief for each case should highlight the key aspects of the case that are relevant for your research problem. Create a short summary of the pertinent facts, holding, and reasoning. Each case brief should include the following:

Citation. Including the full citation will make writing the document easier because you will avoid referring back to the original. Include

---

11. Always be careful when printing statutes from an annotated code. Typically, the default mode of printing code provisions from either Westlaw or Lexis Advance is to print not just the statute itself, but all associated annotations as well. For statutes that have been heavily litigated, printing without changing this default could result in a print job of several hundred pages. Depending on whether your subscription charges for printing by the page or document, this could be a very costly mistake.

parallel cites to give yourself the most flexibility and reduce the likelihood of having to relocate the parallel cites.

Facts. Include only those facts that are relevant to your project.

Procedural posture. State the procedural posture of the case and note any information about the standard of review applied by the court.

Holding and reasoning. Summarize the court's analysis. Again, address only those issues in the case that are relevant to your project. For example, if a case involves a tort claim and the issue of when expert testimony will be admitted in court, and you are researching only the tort issue, there is no need for you to study and summarize the court's reasoning on admission of expert witness testimony. Skim that section to be sure there is no relevant information lurking there, then ignore it.

Pinpoint pages. For case information that you will cite in your written document, include the pinpoint cite. Be sure that the pinpoint is to the page in the reporter that you have been asked to cite in your document, not to a parallel reporter.

Reflections. Include your thoughts on the opinion: How do you anticipate using it in your analysis? Does it resolve certain issues for your problem? Does it raise new questions?

Updating information. Each case brief should have a designated space for updating. Whether you use KeyCite, Shepard's, or BCite, you must update each case that you use in your analysis.

E. Updating

You will likely find yourself updating at several points during the research process. Updating with Shepard's, BCite, or KeyCite early in the process will lead you to other authorities on point. Updating before you begin to rely on an authority is critical: you must verify that each authority you include in your analysis is still "good law." Updating just before submitting a document ensures that nothing has changed while you were working on the project.

F. Outlining Your Analysis[12]

Because the most effective research often occurs in conjunction with the analysis of your particular project, try to develop an outline that addresses

---

12. Sections F and G are drawn from *Oregon Legal Research* and are used with permission.

your client's problem as soon as you can. If outlining feels too restrictive, you may benefit from a chart that organizes all the primary authority by issue or element, such as in Table 8-3, following the typical legal analysis format of Issue-Rule-Application-Conclusion (IRAC).

Your first analytical outline or chart may be based on information in a secondary authority, the requirements of a statute, or the elements of a common law claim. It will become more sophisticated and detailed as you conduct your research. Recognize that you cannot reread every case or statute in its entirety each time you need to include it in your outline; instead, refer to your notes and briefs to find the key ideas supporting each step in your analysis.

The outline or chart should enable you to synthesize the law, apply the law to your client's facts, and reach a conclusion on the desired outcome. Applying the law to your client's facts may lead you to research issues that may not be apparent in your initial assessment of the situation.

Table 8-3. Sample Analysis Chart

Research Question: Is an employee entitled to unemployment compensation after being dismissed from employment because, due to problems with drug addiction, he twice was caught sleeping on the job and threatened the coworker who reported him to the supervisor on the second occasion?

Controlling Statute: Tenn. Code Ann. § 50-7-303(b)

Issue	Case	Rule	Application	Conclusion
Is sleeping on the job "misconduct connected with ... work"?	*Wallace*	Excessive absenteeism may be the basis of a finding of misconduct, but that level of absenteeism is determined on a case-by-case basis.	Sleeping on the job may be analogous to absenteeism	Two instances of sleeping on the job probably will not amount to employee misconduct if the employee was tired due to illness or disability, unless the employee disregarded a warning concerning the conduct or additional circumstances contributed to the dismissal.

Table 8-3. Sample Analysis Chart

Research Question: Is an employee entitled to unemployment compensation after being dismissed from employment because, due to problems with drug addiction, he twice was caught sleeping on the job and threatened the coworker who reported him to the supervisor on the second occasion?

Controlling Statute: Tenn. Code Ann. § 50-7-303(b)

Issue	Case	Rule	Application	Conclusion
	Miotke	Repeated absences by an employee who ignored four warnings that absenteeism would result in termination constituted misconduct connected with employment, even though the absences were related to the employee's alcoholism.	Sleeping had occurred on only two occasions.	
	Trout	Absences due to illness do not constitute misconduct.	Sleeping on the job was related to drug addiction.	

Table 8-3. Sample Analysis Chart

Research Question: Is an employee entitled to unemployment compensation after being dismissed from employment because, due to problems with drug addiction, he twice was caught sleeping on the job and threatened the coworker who reported him to the supervisor on the second occasion?

Controlling Statute: Tenn. Code Ann. § 50-7-303(b)

Issue	Case	Rule	Application	Conclusion
Is threatening a coworker "misconduct connected with … work?"	*Armstrong*	Misconduct must amount to a breach of duty owed to the employer. Threatening a co-worker did not amount to misconduct because the threat was not directed at a supervisor, the incident did not disrupt work, and the employee had not been warned that this type of conduct would result in his immediate discharge.	Employee threatened a co-worker, not a supervisor. Employee had not been warned that threatening co-worker would result in immediate discharge.	In these circumstances, a threat intended to prevent a co-worker from reporting the employee's sleeping on the job may amount to breach of a duty owed to the employer only if it materially interfered with the employer's business.

G. Ending Your Research

One of the most difficult problems new researchers face is deciding when to stop researching. Often deadlines imposed by the court or a supervisor will limit the amount of time spent on a research project. The expense to the client will also be a consideration.

Apart from these practical constraints, most legal researchers want to believe that if they search long enough they will find a case or statute or article or *something* that answers the client's legal question clearly, succinctly, and definitively. Sometimes that happens, but usually it doesn't. So, if you do not experience that *Eureka!* moment of finding the exact answer summed up in one authority, how do you know when your research is over?

The strongest sign that you have come to at least an initial stopping point is that your research in various sources leads you back to the same authorities. For example, say you first find a good, explanatory secondary authority. The secondary authority cites to case opinions and statutes. You look up the statutes in an annotated code, and check the case annotations there. The cases summarized in the annotated code are the same cases that you found cited in the secondary source. Perhaps you find some cross-references to related statutes. You read those, and examine their case annotations. Again, the case summaries are of the same decisions to which you already have citations. You turn to reading the case opinions, and find that they all interpret and apply the statutes you have already read. You update the cases with a citator such as Shepard's or KeyCite, and find that the cases have been cited by some law review articles. You skim the law review articles, and find that they all cite the case opinions and statutes you have already found. Eventually, your research seems to be leading you in a circle, back to where you have already been, rather than branching out to new authorities. This is a strong indication of the thoroughness of your research. As a final checklist, go through each step of the basic research process outlined in Chapter 1 to ensure you considered each one. Then review your research plan and notes on your research process to make sure that you have covered all of the issues presented to you.

When you are working online, knowing when to stop researching can be particularly difficult. Because you are jumping from link to link and database to database without moving from your computer, it is easier to lose track of where you have been online, and what you have seen, than if you are reading books in a library, and moving from one shelf to another, or one volume to another. This is where your careful note-taking will help you immensely. Also, be sure to make use of the history-logging functions on paid commercial research services to review your past searches and viewed documents as a supplement to your research notes.

If you have worked through the research process and found nothing, it may be that nothing exists. Before reaching that conclusion, though, expand your research terms and look in a few more secondary authorities. If you have not already done so, try looking at other jurisdictions to see if they have helpful persuasive primary authority. If they do, you could use it in your work directly, or you could see if it will help bring you closer to authority from your home jurisdiction that you did not find in your earlier research. For example, if you were originally researching Tennessee law, but could only find a relevant case opinion from Georgia, perhaps you would find better search terms within the Georgia case that you could use to refine your searching in a Tennessee case law database.

Remember that the goal of your research is to solve a client's problem. Sometimes the law will not seem to support the solution that your client had in mind. Think creatively to address the client's problem in a different way. While you must tell your supervisor or your client when a desired approach is not feasible, you will want to have prepared an alternate solution if possible.

Appendix A

Where to Find Tennessee Law

Tennessee Cases

Print sources: *West's South Western Reporter, Tennessee Decisions*
- Summaries of some unpublished appellate cases are also available in *Tennessee Attorneys Memo*
- Very old Tennessee cases are available in miscellaneous reporters discussed in Chapter 2.

Free websites:
- http://www.tsc.state.tn.us/—coverage starts in 1995/1996
- http://scholar.google.com—coverage starts in 1950

Lexis Advance:
- Browse → Sources → By Jurisdiction → Tennessee → Cases
- Sample citation formats for retrieving a Tennessee case using the universal search bar:
  136 S.W.2d 721
  2 Tenn. Ch. App. 132
  225 Tenn. 1.

Westlaw:
- Cases → Cases by State → Tennessee.
- Sample citation formats for retrieving a Tennessee case using the universal search bar:
  834 S.W.2d 915
  225 Tenn. 1.

Bloomberg Law:
- Court Opinions → State Court Opinions → Tennessee.
- Sample citation formats for retrieving a Tennessee case using the universal search bar (select Citation Search from drop-down box):
  834 S.W.2d 915
  225 Tenn. 1.

Tennessee Constitution

Print source: *Tennessee Code Annotated* (Michie, official version), *West's Tennessee Code Annotated* (unofficial version)

Free websites:
- http://www.tn.gov/sos/bluebook/11-12/TSS_TNFoundingDocs.pdf (.pdf version provided by the Tennessee Secretary of State)
- http://www.michie.com
  Choose "Tennessee" as your jurisdiction. Use expandable menus to browse to Tennessee Constitution.

Lexis Advance:
- Type *Tennessee Constitution* into the universal search bar to search the constitution or browse the table of contents.
- Sample citation format to retrieve a specific constitutional provision using the universal search bar:
  Tenn. Const. art. I @1

Westlaw:
- Statutes & Court Rules → Tennessee → Constitution of the State of Tennessee.
- Sample citation format to retrieve a specific constitutional provision using the universal search bar:
  TN CONST Art. 1, s 1

Bloomberg Law:
- State Law → Tennessee → Tenn. Legislative → Tennessee Constitution.
- Sample citation format to retrieve a specific constitutional provision using the universal search bar:
  TN CONST Art. 1, sec. 1

Current Statutory Code

Print sources: *Tennessee Code Annotated* (Michie, official version), *West's Tennessee Code Annotated* (unofficial version)

Free website: www.michie.com
- Choose "Tennessee" from alphabetical list of codes
- Unannotated & unofficial

Lexis Advance:
- Type *Tennessee Code Annotated* into the universal search bar to search the code or browse the table of contents.
- Sample format to retrieve a current statute using Get a Document:
  tca 39-1-101

Westlaw:
- Statutes & Court Rules → Tennessee
- Sample citation format to retrieve a specific statute using the universal search bar:
  tn st 39-11-101

Bloomberg Law:
- State Law → Tennessee → Tenn. Legislative → Tennessee Code
- Code is unannotated but has a built-in search feature to retrieve cases citing specific code sections
- Sample citation format to retrieve a specific statute using the universal search bar:
  tn code 39-11-101

Archival/Superseded Statutory Codes

Print sources: Check with your law library to see if it maintains archived versions in print or on microfiche.

Free website: None.

Lexis Advance:
- From home page, scroll down to Archives pane. Archived Code Search → Codes → Jurisdiction → Tennessee.
- Coverage begins in 1991.
- If you have retrieved a current code section, you can access archived versions of it by clicking "Archived Code Versions" on the right side of the page.

Westlaw:
- Statutes & Court Rules → Tennessee → Tennessee Statute Annotated— Historical.
- Coverage begins in 2001.
- If you have retrieved a current code section, you can access historical versions of it by clicking the "History" tab.

Bloomberg Law: archived codes are not available on Bloomberg Law.

Session Laws/Slip Laws

Print source: *Public and Private Acts of the State of Tennessee* (ceased publication in 2006).

Free government website: http://sos.tn.gov/division-publications/acts-and-resolutions.
- Coverage begins in 1997.

- May be browsed by chapter number or searched by title, bill number, or abstract.

Lexis Advance:
- To search: Browse → Sources → By Jurisdiction → Tennessee → Category → Statutes and Legislation → Tennessee Advance Legislative Service.
- Coverage begins in 1989.
- Sample format to retrieve a Tennessee session law using the universal search bar:
  1997 Tenn. Pub Acts 244

Westlaw:
- To search: type Tennessee Historical Enacted Legislation into the universal search bar to locate session laws prior to the current session. Type Tennessee Enacted Legislation into the universal search bar to locate session laws from the current legislative session.
- Coverage begins in 1990.
- It is not possible to retrieve a Tennessee session law using a citation in the universal search bar.

Bloomberg Law:
- To search: State Law → Tennessee → Tenn. Legislative → Tennessee Public and Private Acts.
- Coverage begins in 1999.
- It is not possible to retrieve a Tennessee session law using a citation in the universal search bar.

Administrative Code

Print source: not available in print.

Free government website: http://sos.tn.gov/effective-rules
- This online version is the official version.
- The regulations are in .pdf format; they are not easily searchable.

Lexis Advance:
- To search or browse: Browse → Sources → By Jurisdiction → Tennessee → Category → Administrative Codes and Regulations.
- Archived versions may be accessed by clicking the "Archived Code Versions" link on the right side of the regulation display screen. Coverage begins in 2004.
- Sample format to retrieve a Tennessee regulation using the universal search bar:
  Tenn. Comp. R. & Regs. R. 1720-4-6.01

Westlaw:
- To search or browse: State Materials → Tennessee → Tennessee Regulations.
- To access archived versions of regulations, type Tennessee Historical Regulations into the universal search bar. Coverage begins in 2002.
- Sample citation format to retrieve a Tennessee regulation using the universal search bar: Tenn. Comp. R. & Regs. 0400-15-01-.13.

Bloomberg Law:
- To search or browse: State Law → Tennessee → Tenn. Regulatory & Administrative → Tennessee Rules & Regulations.
- Sample citation format to retrieve a Tennessee regulation using the universal search bar: Tenn. Comp. R. & Regs. 0400-15-01-.13 [citation search].

Administrative Register (Pending or Proposed Rules)
Pending Regulations

Print source: not available in print.

Free government website: http://sos.tn.gov/products/division-publications/administrative-register
- The online version is the official version.
- This free online version is typically more current than versions available elsewhere.

Lexis Advance: current pending regulations are not available on Lexis Advance.

Westlaw:
- State Materials → Tennessee → Tennessee Regulations → Tennessee Proposed & Adopted Regulations
- It is not possible to retrieve a proposed regulation using a citation in the universal search bar.

Bloomberg Law:
- State Materials → Tennessee → Tennessee Regulations → Tennessee Proposed & Adopted Regulations
- It is not possible to retrieve a proposed regulation using a citation in the universal search bar.

Tennessee Court Rules, Evidentiary Rules, Procedural Rules, and Professional Rules

Print sources: Tennessee court rules and professional rules are included in the "Rules" volumes of the *Tennessee Code Annotated* and *West's Tennessee Code*

Annotated. The Rules of Professional Conduct for attorneys are found at Rule 8 in the Tennessee Supreme Court Rules. The Rules volumes also include selected Local Rules of Practice.

Free government website: http://www.tncourts.gov/courts/rules.
- This site also includes links to proposed rules.
- All rule sets may be searched together using the search box on the lower right side of the page.

Lexis Advance:
- To search or browse: Browse → Sources → By Jurisdiction → Tennessee → Category: Statutes and Legislation → Tennessee Local, State & Federal Rules
- Sample citation format to retrieve a specific rule using the universal search bar: Tenn. R. Crim. P. RULE 3

Westlaw:
- To search or browse: Statutes and Court Rules → Tennessee → State and Local Rules
- To retrieve a Tennessee rule of court with a known citation, type *Tennessee Court Rules Find Template* into the universal search bar.

Bloomberg Law:
- To search or browse: State Law → Tennessee → Tenn. Court Rules
- Sample citation format to retrieve a Tennessee court rule using the universal search bar: Tenn. R. Evid. 501 [Citation Search].

Attorney General Opinions

Print source: *Opinions of the Attorney General of the State of Tennessee.* Ceased publication in print in 2000.

Free government website: http://www.tn.gov/attorneygeneral/topic/attorney-general-opinions
- Searchable or browseable
- Available 1999 (partial) to present

Lexis Advance:
- To search: type Tennessee Attorney General Opinions into universal search bar, then "add source as filter." Coverage starts in 1977.
- It is not possible to retrieve an attorney general opinion using a known citation on Lexis Advance.

Westlaw:
- To search: type Tennessee Attorney General Opinions into the universal search bar. Coverage starts in 1977.

- Sample citation to retrieve a Tennessee Attorney General opinion using the universal search bar: Tenn. Op. Atty. Gen. No. 01-156
  Note that *01* in this sample citation refers to the year of publication (2001), noted as a two-digit number.

Bloomberg Law:
- To search: State Law → Tennessee → Tenn. Agents and Departments → Tennessee Office of the Attorney General → Opinions. Coverage starts in 2000.
- It is not possible to retrieve an attorney general opinion using a citation on Bloomberg Law.

Appendix B

Selected Bibliography

General Research (tending to focus on federal material)

Mary Garvey Algero, *Federal Legal Research* (2d ed. 2015).

Steven Barken, et al., *Fundamentals of Legal Research* (10th ed. 2015).

Stephen Elias, *Legal Research : How to Find and Understand the Law* (16th ed. 2012).

Christina L. Kunz et al., *The Process of Legal Research* (8th ed. 2012).

Ruth Ann McKinney & Scott Childs, *Legal Research: A Practical Guide and Self-Instructional Workbook* (5th ed. 2008).

Kent C. Olson, *Legal Research in a Nutshell* (11th ed. 2013).

Mark Osbeck, *Impeccable Research, A Concise Guide to Mastering Legal Research Skills* (2d ed. 2015).

Amy E. Sloan, *Basic Legal Research: Tools and Strategies* (5d ed. 2012).

Tennessee Research

Lewis L. Laska, *Tennessee Legal Research Handbook* (1977).

Ann Walsh Long & Sibyl Marshall, *Find It Free & Fast on the Net: Strategies for Legal Research on the Web* (2015).

Steven R. Thorpe, Uncovering Legislative History Resources in Tennessee, 31 *Tenn. B.J.* 18 (1995).

Specialized and Advanced Legal Research

J.D.S. Armstrong & Christopher A. Knott, *Where the Law Is: An Introduction to Advanced Legal Research* (4th ed. 2012).

Prestatehood Legal Materials: A Fifty-State Research Guide, Including New York City and the District of Columbia (Michael Chiorazzi & Marguerite Most eds., 2005).

George Washington International Law Review, *Guide to International Legal Research* (2015).

Specialized Legal Research (Penny A. Hazleton ed., 2005) (looseleaf).

William A. Raabe et al., *Federal Tax Research* (9th ed. 2012).

About the Authors

Scott Childs is Professor and Associate Dean for Library & Technology Services at the University of Tennessee College of Law.

Sibyl Marshall is Associate Professor and the Head of Public Services at the University of Tennessee's Joel A. Katz Law Library.

Carol McCrehan Parker is the Assistant Vice President for Faculty Affairs at Emerson College, and was formerly the Associate Dean for Academic Affairs, an Associate Professor of Law, and Director of Legal Writing at the University of Tennessee College of Law.

Index